T0295977

Pseudo-Authenticity and Tourism

This book explores the concept of authenticity in tourism through the analysis of six tourist sites in Guangdong Province and Macau, China.

Through a review of tourism literature, it develops the concept of pseudo-authenticity in which tourist sites and cultural products function to give signs of authenticity for tourists. This is achieved through the influence of media, authentic fakery, and façadism. Readers will gain greater insight into tourist sites in China that operate through cultural preservation, the miniaturization of cultural assets, and the replication of foreign signs through reproductions of foreign cities. The authors outline the tourist sites, an aesthetic analysis, on-site interviews with tourists, and an examination of online reviews of the sites.

This is a useful work for scholars and students of tourism studies in China and around the world, especially those concerned with issues of authenticity and the effects of commodification on cultural assets.

Jesse Owen Hearns-Branaman is Associate Professor of International Journalism and the Head of the Department of Communication at Beijing Normal University – Hong Kong Baptist University United International College.

Andy Lihua Chen is a PhD candidate in Communication of the joint research postgraduate programme of Beijing Normal University – Hong Kong Baptist University United International College and Hong Kong Baptist University.

Routledge Insights in Tourism Series
Series Editor
Anukrati Sharma
Head & Associate Professor of the Department of Commerce and Management at the University of Kota, India

This series provides a forum for cutting edge insights into the latest developments in tourism research. It offers high quality monographs and edited collections that develop tourism analysis at both theoretical and empirical levels.

Management of Tourism Ecosystem Services in a Post Pandemic Context
Global Perspectives
Edited by Vanessa G. B. Gowreesunkar, Shem Wambugu Maingi and Felix Lamech Mogambi Ming'ate

Tourism, Knowledge and Learning
Conceptual Development and Case Studies
Edited by Eva Maria Jernsand, Maria Persson and Erik Lundberg

Potentials, Challenges and Prospects of Halal Tourism Development in Ethiopia
Mohammed Jemal Ahmed and Atilla Akbaba

Diasporic Mobilities on Vacation
Tourism of European-Moroccans at Home
Lauren B Wagner

Overtourism and Cruise Tourism in Emerging Destinations on the Arabian Peninsula
Manuela Gutberlet

Pseudo-Authenticity and Tourism
Preservation, Miniaturization, and Replication
Jesse Owen Hearns-Branaman and Andy Lihua Chen

For more information about this series, please visit: www.routledge.com/Routledge-Insights-in-Tourism-Series/book-series/RITS

Pseudo-Authenticity and Tourism

Preservation, Miniaturization, and Replication

Jesse Owen Hearns-Branaman and Andy Lihua Chen

LONDON AND NEW YORK

First published 2024
by Routledge
4 Park Square, Milton Park, Abingdon, Oxon OX14 4RN

and by Routledge
605 Third Avenue, New York, NY 10158

Routledge is an imprint of the Taylor & Francis Group, an informa business

British Library Cataloguing-in-Publication Data
A catalogue record for this book is available from the British Library

ISBN: 978-1-032-27210-8 (hbk)
ISBN: 978-1-032-27211-5 (pbk)
ISBN: 978-1-003-29181-7 (ebk)

DOI: 10.4324/9781003291817

Typeset in Times New Roman
by Apex CoVantage, LLC

Contents

About the Authors

Jesse Owen Hearns-Branaman is Associate Professor of International Journalism and the Head of the Department of Communication at Beijing Normal University – Hong Kong Baptist University United International College. His research interests include poststructuralism, ideology, critical linguistics, political economy of news, comparative journalism, tourism, and epistemological theory. He has published two books: *Journalism and the Philosophy of Truth: Beyond Objectivity and Balance* (Routledge, 2016) and *The Political Economy of News in China: Manufacturing Harmony* (Lexington, 2015), and one edited volume, *Journalism and Foreign Policy: How the US and UK Media Cover Official Enemies* (Routledge, 2022).

Andy Lihua Chen is a PhD candidate in Communication of the joint research postgraduate programme of Beijing Normal University–Hong Kong Baptist University United International College and Hong Kong Baptist University. His primary research interests include fandom/anti-fandom, popular culture and the culture industry, tourism, and discourse analysis, from both sociocultural and critical perspectives. He is interested in looking at how people make sense of the media texts, content, and cultures in relation to their own social background. His PhD dissertation explores anti-fans' reception of and reaction to Chinese pop stars from a Bourdieuian perspective.

Figures

Acknowledgements

The authors would like to thank their families, colleagues, and each other for their support during the preparation of the book. We would also like to thank Prachi Priyanka, Chris Parry, Faye Leerink, and everyone at Routledge for their kind assistance.

Financial contribution to the project was provided by the Research Development and Knowledge Transfer Office of Beijing Normal University–Hong Kong Baptist University United International College.

1 Introduction

Waiting in the shuttle station at the top of Mt Emei in Sichuan Province, a video is playing on the small TV hanging from the ceiling in the corner of the station. The video shows all the highlights of a trip to Sichuan Province: the Giant Buddha statue carved into the side of a cliff in Leshan, the beautiful sunrise you can view from the top of Mt Emei during good weather, and playful pandas running around their enclosures in one of the various breeding centres across the province.

Then, a more surprising image comes on a group of people farming, picking crops in the field, all while wearing their elegant and distinctive ethnic clothing. Their outfits are certainly beautiful and unique and do show that ethnic group's style and aesthetics. Yet it begs the question: do people really farm in clothing that is clearly ceremonial and likely to be only worn on special occasions? Why was a decision made to represent them in such an odd way?

Showing people in this manner does not function to illustrate to prospective tourists what the actual authentic life of those people is like, nor what we would experience if we travelled there. It functions, in the logic of media and advertising, to give signs of that ethnic group, to show there is some difference between them and the target audience, in this case tourists from all over China, and to show that by visiting there you will cross some kind of boundary into an exotic world where things are not the same. Certainly, you may have seen people farming before, but to really show how *different* this place is, you need to give even more evidence, signs of ethnicity, and a sense of exoticism.

Anyone who has travelled around the world has run into these kinds of confusing experiences regarding the authenticity of culture. Cohen mentions an anecdote of a teacher travelling in northern Thailand whose "sense of cultural authenticity" was "offended" by the tribal village's usage of "industrially produced plastic cups instead of indigenously produced bamboo cups" (Cohen 1988, p. 378). Yet, the tribe 'authentically' used plastic cups, probably because they are cheap and convenient and there is no longer a need to make ones from bamboo. If they did make bamboo cups for tourists to buy, would that still be authentic?

DOI: 10.4324/9781003291817-1

Authentic thus means a cup made of bamboo; inauthentic means a mass-produced cup made of plastic; hyperreal means a mass-produced cup made of plastic that looks like bamboo. Some tourists

> will accept a commercialized object as 'authentic,' insofar as they are convinced that it is indeed ornamented with 'traditional' designs and 'hand made' by members of an ethnic group (even though it may have been made of different materials or in a different form than the 'traditional' product and was produced expressly for the market).
>
> (Cohen 1988, p. 378)

Communities, be they ethnic minority groups facing domestic travellers or ordinary people facing international travellers, constantly have to deal with this conundrum. More or less, modernity has spread to all corners of the world and these kinds of exotic 'native' cultural artefacts are being replaced by mass-produced consumer products. If we spend our hard-earned money and time to travel to distant places only to find they are very similar to our own lives, then what is the point of all this effort and expenditure of resources?

In the following research, we hope to answer these questions and more concerning authenticity in contemporary tourism. Our focus is specifically on tourist sites in China, Guangdong Province and Macau, which have special relationships to authenticity. We will look at sites that are supposedly preserving authentic culture, sites that attempt to represent China and the world through miniatures, and sites that claim to reproduce foreign cities. Before we get to that, we first will explore the major areas of tourism research.

How to Study Tourism?

There are a multiplicity of perspectives taken when studying tourism and tourists. Here, we will look at four of the main aspects, beginning with looking at the needs of tourists. Then, we will turn to the rise of modernity and class and its relationship with tourism as colonialism and globalization. Finally, we will consider sustainable approaches to cultural heritage assets. This is done to give the background of tourism outside of specific talk of authenticity and will underpin the discussions of authenticity in the next chapter.

Tourists' Needs

Tourists partake in tourism for some reason, and the investment of our time, money, and other resources to travel short term for reasons other than work or education thus must fulfil some kinds of needs. McKercher and du Cros argue that tourism "sells dreams and experiences that satisfy the consumer's needs, wants and desires," such as "to have an inner need satisfied," no matter if the experience is "deep or shallow" (McKercher and du Cros 2002, p. 106). These needs can be about educating ourselves on new cultures or foreign cultures we are moderately familiar with but want to explore in a more direct and deep way. This includes partaking in cultural activities such as music or dance that we cannot access at home, eating exotic food made directly by the people who developed it, or viewing art, architecture, sculpture, famous buildings, and the like face-to-face. They can be just about getting away to somewhere other than where we are all the time, to rest and relax so we can go back to our everyday lives with renewed vigour. They can be rituals, such as honeymoons or graduation trips. They can be spiritual, pilgrimages to religious sites, or, more frequently in the era of social media, pilgrimages to those famous places we always see pop up on our feeds.

Yet these kinds of needs have not always existed or at least the means to be able to meet those needs has not been accessible to the masses until very recently. Tourism is a wholly modern endeavour different from travel and intricately tied to class.

Modernity and Class

The earliest forms of what would become tourism developed in Europe in the Middle Ages with Christian pilgrimages to Rome and the Middle East, specifically Jerusalem. In this, there developed a small industry serving the travellers, such as developing rudimentary maps, but the overall impact was quite minimal. After the Renaissance, travel as a rite of passage for elite young men grew in popularity. This developed into an almost standardized Grand Tour in the seventeenth to eighteenth centuries. During these travels, the young men, chaperoned by an older experienced relative, would travel to France, Switzerland, Germany, and Italy, specifically Rome and Venice. These travels, however, depended on already existing socio-political networks of the nobility across Europe who would facilitate each other's travel and accommodation, hosting the young travellers as part of their social obligations. The tour could last for years in total, with months spent in each destination, which facilitated deeper experiences for the travellers in learning about the culture, habits, customs, and languages of the different areas of Europe.

This was far from the modern profit-oriented commercialized tourist industry, but it still forms the skeleton for much of modern cultural tourism, such as guidebooks, travel literature, visiting famous sites, and experiencing local culture. In many ways, modern tourism is a commercialized and truncated version of the Grand Tour; relationships between locals and natives are based on monetary, not social, relationships, and the length of travel has to be limited to the tourists' budget. Interestingly, the social obligation for some young middle-class people to travel to the same kinds of places still exists, such as in students taking gap years abroad.

As Urry and Larson (2011, pp. 34–36) illustrate, tourism in the UK grew in the nineteenth century due to the increase in the working-class population which had moved to urban areas and had more disposable income yet lived in very crowded urban living conditions quite at odds with the rural environment they were used to. Travel to seaside resorts, for example, by the newly urbanized populations allowed them to revitalize and spend their hard-earned money. As the number of tourists increased, services increased as well to meet their needs, with games and other cultural activities developed accordingly. Having weekends off work meant that "holidays should be taken *en masse* and celebrated by the whole community" (Walton 1978, p. 35). This led to the creation of a sort of tourism culture based on getting away from the city and participating in relaxing activities that did not tax the mind and allowed them to recoup energy to continue working after the holiday ended.

The creation of travel agencies and package tours started in the mid-nineteenth century in the UK, generally attributed to Thomas Cook. He first started organizing tour groups within the UK and eventually spread the business to Europe, specifically Italy, and eventually the USA, the Middle East, and Egypt (see Hom 2015). This innovated many now standard features, such as organized tour groups with a set schedule to ensure all the main spots are visited, group booking of hotels and transportation to get discounts, and coupons for certain shops. This allowed a greater segment of society to participate in tourism, especially those without a lot of previous knowledge about the destination, as money and time were the only things needed to be able to participate.

While it started in "the industrialized Western countries in the 19th century," tourism as a leisure activity eventually "spread to other parts of the world, especially to the affluent classes of poor countries" (van den Berghe 1980, p. 375). We can thus see how it is also intimately connected to notions of class, it "presupposes affluence" because "it serves no purpose other than recreational, and it is expensive and time consuming" (van den Berghe 1980, p. 375). Everyone can participate in *some* level of tourism, as MacCannell puts it: "Modernity is breaking up the 'leisure class,' capturing its fragments and distributing them to everyone" (MacCannell 1976, p. 37). This is why the scope of tourism does not simply include travel to far away distant foreign places, as was the norm for elites in Europe in the pre-modern era, but also includes travel to closer local or regional areas.

In the end, we have a wide gap between pre-modern travelling and tourism, or as Baudrillard puts it: "Nothing is further from pure travelling than tourism or holiday travel" (Baudrillard 1989, p. 9). Further, modern tourism is a cultural invention and "most definitely not something natural or innate" (Crang 2004, pp. 78–79). It is "a set of learned competencies and skills" (Crang 2004, pp. 78–79) that we get from our environment, from media, from education, from our friends and family and co-workers and classmates. The knowledge of tourists in mass tourism is under question too, as Boorstin says, because "[t]he tourist looks for caricature; travel agents at home and national tourist bureaus abroad are quick to oblige" (Boorstin 1961, p. 106).

While mass tourism may be democratized and institutionalized as a typical and even expected behaviour, its foundations still lie in the middle class or working class and modernization. Many cultural tourists who visit "heritage attractions seem to be seeking affirmation of how modern they are and how much modern society has evolved from the past" (du Cros and McKercher 2015, p. 117)

Not all classes can participate in tourism, yet the amount of people around the world who can participate, especially in developing countries like China, has increased dramatically in the last 40 years. Pre-pandemic, in 2019, the travel and tourism industry contributed 11.6% to the GDP of China, up from 9.4% in 2014 (Statista 2023a). In 2019, 155 million Chinese travelled abroad, triple the numbers from 2010 (Statista 2023b).

Colonialism and Globalization

The influence of the imperialist and colonialist stages of European history should not be ignored when discussing modern tourism. Although there is no space for an entire review here, we will emphasize the specific influences this had on the development of modern tourism.

In the age of discovery, Europeans travelled around the world, enslaving and exploiting populations. Simultaneously, Europeans started to view their culture in juxtaposition to these foreign cultures, sometimes with disdain, sometimes with curiosity, but always with an air of superiority (see Said 1989). European powers involved in these colonial endeavours started a concentrated campaign to bring back artefacts from these cultures around the world, as trophies of victories in combat and as objects of curiosity. These artefacts would be stored in individual's domiciles, ready for display to their guests to show off their accomplishments.

For example, from 1798 to 1801, Napoleon's forces temporarily conquered parts of the middle east from the Ottoman Empire, specifically Egypt. This led to the discovery of artefacts such as the Rosetta Stone and the creation of many great works on Egyptology, such as the *Description de l'Égypte*, and the popularization of Egypt, the Pyramids, the Sphinx, and other monuments in the minds of Europeans. This, and other factors, led to the growth of tourism in Europe in the nineteenth century. Although it was largely limited to the elite classes, the growth of tour agencies, as discussed earlier, certainly opened up the ability to travel to exotic locations more easily.

This caused the growth in services for European tourists, such as hotels and restaurants to suit their tastes. It also led to massive looting of shrines and graves by the locals to retrieve authentic artefacts to sell to the tourists. Eventually, this supply ran out, so the locals then turned to creating replicas of the artefacts, tricking tourists into believing they were real in order to earn more money. Eventually, many artefacts ended up, by various means, to museums and art galleries to allow for more public display or to universities for archaeological study. This, in turn, necessitated the ability to verify whether the artefacts were authentic or fake.

Researchers such as Hom (2010) and Rosaldo (1989) argue that much tourism is based on remnants of colonialism and imperialism and thus is motivated in a large part by nostalgia for that what has been lost. Colonization and modernization feature the destruction and transformation of that what came before, and those who colonized and modernized feel a sense of responsibility and loss and hence nostalgia, and feel a need to revisit what is gone. This includes one's own culture as well as other cultures and is not just from Europe and the West to the rest of the world. As Urry and Larson point out, "rising incomes for an Asian middle class (as well as the student study tour and 'backpacker tourism') have generated a strong desire to see those places of the west that appear to define global culture" (Urry and Larson 2011, p. 25). As Sakwit (2021, p. 50). argues,

> With globalization, culture is not there to make a singular difference in each place. Instead, the recreation of culture in a local place for tourists causes the distinction between real culture and contrived/staged culture to disappear. What is globalized in tourism, therefore, refers to the erosion of the difference between real culture and simulated culture.

Thus, "the boundary of the global and the local" has become "blurred" in that "the global cannot be realized without a local context" and, at the same time, "the idea of the local . . . accords with the global" (Sakwit 2021, p. 47).

As with modernization, colonialism and globalization are a heavy influence on tourism, giving us the motivation to not only learn and consume signs about our own culture but others as well. This is heavily couched in terms of consuming the other, the foreigner or the exotic, and images from the past.

Sustainability of Cultural Assets

A more recent trend is concern about the sustainability of tourism, in other words, how mass tourism itself may harm and eventually destroy the tangible and intangible cultural heritage assets that attract tourists. Promoting tourism in communities can have massive benefits to the economy and development of the area. Cultural tourism "provides an opportunity to position communities uniquely and, in doing so, gain a sustainable competitive advantage" (du Cros and McKercher 2015, p. 3).

This requires coordination and planning by multiple stakeholders, such as the locals, government agencies, and NGOs. "Access must be managed carefully to ensure that the tangible values of the asset are not damaged or the intangible values compromised" (du Cros and McKercher 2015, pp. 50–51).

UNESCO defines intangible cultural heritage as "practices, representations, expressions, knowledge and skills" that are "transmitted from generation to generation, is constantly recreated by communities and groups in response to their environment, their interaction with nature and their history, and provides them with a sense of identity and continuity" (UNESCO 2003, p. §1 article 2.1). The convention goes on to define ICH as "(a) oral traditions and expressions, including language as a vehicle of the intangible cultural heritage; (b) performing arts; (c) social practices, rituals and festive events; (d) knowledge and practices concerning nature and the universe; (e) traditional craftsmanship."

Both intangible and tangible cultural heritage needs to be preserved, and such culture that is under threat from modernization and urbanization needs to be the subject of special attention. As mentioned, one way to do so is to promote sustainable tourism in certain places. McKercher and du Cros provide a list of the kinds of features that such places "with tourism potential share" (McKercher and du Cros 2002, p. 33):

- "known beyond the local heritage community"
- "provide experiences that can be consumed"
- "are interesting and unique"
- "are robust" and "can absorb visitation"
- "are accessible" and
- "provide the tourist with some compelling reason to visit"

The promotion of a kind of "cultural space" is also very important to consider as it "allows all kinds of intangible assets to be associated with a traditional setting that enhances the interpretation and absorption of the asset's cultural values by the visitor" (du Cros and McKercher 2015, p. 174). As we will discuss more in the next chapter, the maintenance of cultural spaces in which both tangible and intangible cultures can interact in a sustainable way is hard to manage and in many cases impossible to maintain due to being transformed into tourism assets.

Tourists and Authenticity

The main issue we will discuss in this book is that of authenticity. While not directly implicated in the aforementioned discussion, authenticity is an implicit and integral part of most cultural tourism. If modern tourists have a need to explore and learn about other cultures, it should be authentic culture, otherwise what is the point? Yet the relationship between tourists and authenticity is a very contested area. Du Cros and McKercher (2015, p. 106) argued that "Tourists want 'authenticity' but not necessarily reality"; this was then updated in the next edition of their book to say "Tourists want authentic experiences, but do not necessarily want to experience reality" (du Cros and McKercher 2020, p. 144).

Studies have found if tourists feel their experience is authentic then that is "a strong indicator of their intention to revisit" (Park *et al.* 2019, p. 99). This then has a knock-on effect on the reputation of the site spread by word of mouth and on social media. Certainly, a tourist site that everyone says feels authentic has beneficial effects on visitation, and conversely, one could argue the opposite.

Yet others argue that authenticity means little to tourists. Cultural tourism "will attract nonlocal visitors (or tourists) who are travelling primarily for pleasure on limited budgets and who may know little about the significance of the assets being visited" (McKercher and du Cros 2002, p. 7). Several researchers even argue that heritage tourists in fact demand and require a certain level of staging of authenticity. Chhabra et al., for example, purport that "staging need not preclude authenticity" because "what is staged is not superficial" in that it "contains elements of the original tradition" (Chhabra *et al.* 2003, p. 715). Surveys found tourists simply "enjoyed seeing new things in the [floating] market," that it was an "enjoyable experience," and the tourists "did not even pay attention to what was real or unreal" (Sakwit 2021, p. 133). If the authenticity or realness/unrealness of the place is irrelevant to the tourist, then why does the tourist site make so much effort to give off signs of traditional culture?

Tourists may also reject experiences that are too authentic. Du Cros and McKercher (2015, p. 117) point out that negative aspects of history, such as "pollution, oppression, poor sewerage, and indifferent maintenance of some landscapes" is something that tourists cannot "easily put in context" without more historical knowledge, and "would be considered 'overkill' by tourists," who thus accept the more 'idyllic' manner in which historical sites are presented. Tourism is for leisure and casual contemplation of culture more often than not, and a challenging view of history and the implications of colonialism, for example, are not enjoyable for a wide audience. There are exceptions; for example, museums about genocide and slavery, but they attract a more specific audience who know what they are getting into.

An easy cop-out would be to say that it simply depends on the tourists and their needs and their anticipated experience. Tourists can "conceive 'authenticity' in different degrees of strictness" in that "individuals who are less concerned with the authenticity of their touristic experiences, will be more prepared to accept as 'authentic' a cultural product or attraction which more concerned tourists, applying stricter criteria, will reject as 'contrived'" (Cohen 1988, p. 376).

The point is not necessarily to ask "why do tourists need authenticity" nor to examine how it has been used but, instead, "what does authenticity do?" (Rickly-Boyd 2012, pp. 269–270, Bendix 1997, p. 21). For cultural and heritage tourism, authenticity does a lot. First, it forms the basis and rationale for tourists to go to that location. In the context of China, going to a Chinese heritage tourist site teaches you about your own history, culture, and the ways of life of your ancestors. For Western cultural tourist sites, it teaches you about tangible and intangible culture, foreign cultures, history, and ways of life of people from around the world, and so on. If these sites are biased and unfactual or 'inauthentic' and the visitor will learn inaccurate culture and history, then why visit them? Historical buildings and sites tend to go through expensive renovations and other kinds of work after their original purpose is finished in order to make them acceptable tourist sites (Staples 1995). However, does this process necessarily lead to the spread of inauthentic culture and history? More importantly, is this important to the tourists who visit those sites?

Tourism and Authenticity in China

Generally speaking, tourism research about China is either very general (i.e. Oakes 1998; Li *et al.* 2008) or focused on the authenticity of ethnic tourism, for example in Hainan (Xie 2003; Xie and Wall 2002; Yang and Wall 2009). Specific studies about authenticity in cultural and heritage sites in Guangdong and Macau are far less frequent. Foreign studies on cultural tourism mainly focus on heritage sites tourism, in terms of sustainable development, influence of heritage tourism, development of heritage tourism, values of heritage tourism, and so forth. Domestic studies on cultural tourism mainly focus on sustainable development issues (Zhu and Lu 2005).

Gao and Zheng (2010) argued that in the period of 2005–2006 domestic studies of Chinese tourism started to improve in terms of research range and methods, as compared to the first period of 1999–2004 when most were qualitative discussions. They pointed to Tian (2005) as the turning point to being more quantitative. In that study, Tian (2005) looked at the performances of the Dai ethnic group in Xishuangbanna. Tian's analysis "indicates tourists all think that the dressing of the performers, the performance content, music instrument, the atmosphere, basic posture, the performers' expression and definition of the preside are elements which have the most important impact on the authenticity" (Tian 2005, p. 12). By contrast, the demographics of performers, performance location, language of the singing, and style of the clothes (i.e. formal and ceremonial vs actual daily clothing) did not matter for perceptions of authenticity (Tian 2005, p. 12).

A lot of research is theoretically based on Wang (1999) and the concept of 'existential authenticity.' Chen and Chen (2021) test the influence of different 'tourism commercial symbol[s]' on 'tourist experiential authenticity', which includes objectivism experiential authenticity, constructivism experiential authenticity, and existential experiential authenticity. Jin *et al.* (2022) quantitative study finds that objective authenticity and existential authenticity of traditional villages have a positive impact on tourists' environmentally responsible behaviours.

Chao and Wang (2021) explore the influence of authenticity perception on tourist attitudes and find the more authentic they feel about the site, the more likely they are dependent on, identified with, and loyal to the site. Chen and

Table 1.1 Research topics (Chen and Su 2012, translated by authors)

	Foreign	*Domestic*
Authenticity theories	Classic theory: explain classic theories with new theories; explain new phenomena with classic theories Establishing new theories: explain authenticity with new theories; discuss the necessity of authenticity as a disciplinary concept	Classic theory: proposed existentialism authenticity; learn, compare, and utilize classic theories New theories: very little
Authenticity and tourism protective development	Protection: high official attention, sufficient official documentations, facilitating the evaluation of authenticity and protection; academia realizes the importance of protection but suggests not to over-emphasize protection Development: explore the intrinsic developmental conflict of the current development modes and phenomena; attentive to the internal mechanism	Protection: lack of official attention, very little official documentations or rather general; academia realizes the importance of protection but suggests not to over-emphasize protection Development: focus on phenomena, offer suggestions on the specific phenomenon (particularly the negative influence); discuss development modes
Authenticity and tourism management	Tourist behaviour: the relationships between motives and authenticity; tourists' extrinsic behaviours Tourist experience: criteria of authentic experience; ways of obtaining authentic experience; drawing on new perspectives to explain tourist experience	Tourist behaviour: the relationships between motives and authenticity Tourist experience: the criteria for evaluating authenticity and influential factors of perception in tourist experience; propose new perspectives to explain tourist experience
Authenticity and tourism development	Commercialization: neutral scholars studying the relationships between commercialization and authenticity and exploring the influence and causes of commercialization; positive scholars exploring the benefits of commercialization Authenticity development: the need of authenticity by future tourists; exploring ways of developing authenticity	Commercialization: neutral scholars studying the relationships between commercialization and authenticity and exploring the influence and causes of commercialization; positive scholars exploring the benefits of commercialization

Zhou (2018), by contrast, bring in Waterman's (2007) concepts of 'hedonic' and 'eudaimonic' well-being, that is the sense of enjoyment and happiness vs self-realization of happiness respectively, to better define Wang's (1999) existential authenticity. This does not align with Chen and Zhou's (2018) findings, nor do they reference each other. The difference is in whether existential authenticity positively affects tourist loyalty. Chao and Wang (2021) use "place dependence" and "place identity" as mediators, while Chen and Zhou (2018) use "hedonic well-being" and "eudaimonic well-being" as mediators.

Ma (2020) found the supportive attitudes towards tourism development in ethnic villages heavily depend on perceptions of cultural authenticity and place attachment. Sun (2020) found that both objective and existential authenticity have a significant positive impact on place attachment. "Among the three dimensions of authenticity, construction authenticity and reference authenticity have a stronger predictive effect on local identity and behavioral intention, while objective authenticity has a smaller predictive effect" (Du and Zha 2021, p. 28). Wang (2001) found that when perceptions of objective authenticity are high that affects the satisfaction of tourists, especially in regard to the ancient city's landscape, architecture, and infrastructure.

Gao and Zheng (2010) examined Phoenix Ancient Village in Hunan Province about a variety of tangible and intangible cultural assets, such as ethnic costumes, architecture, food, and historical sites. They surveyed both local residents and tourists on their perception of importance and authenticity and found similar variance between what residents and tourists felt was and was not necessary to improve (Gao and Zheng 2010). Wang and Chen (2022) studied the site Yunnan Ethnic Village in Kunming. They argue that the representation of the ethnic culture is too selective and incomplete. For example, for the Achang nationality, only the Achang architecture and knives are present, but folk music, musical instruments, and dance are absent.

Other studies have noted the negative effects of commercialization on Chinese tourist sites. Zhou and Yu (2004) reported that all respondents found that the inclusion of tourism-related facilities in a natural landscape decreases the quality of the aesthetic value, in this case of a park including a unique landscape of quartz stone. Zhong *et al.* (2009, p. 65) found that increased commercialization caused a loss of naturalness in the tourist site, and thus "those who come to seek the authenticity of being close to nature may turn to other places after their first visitation."

Park *et al.* (2019, p. 105) found that "tourist satisfaction on the authenticity in cultural heritage tourism does not directly affect the conative loyalty that influences their future behavioral intention; but it affects formation of conative loyalty via cognitive and affective loyalties." Yang and Wall (2009), by contrast, conducted extensive quantitative surveys in Xishuangbanna, Yunnan, finding that Chinese tourists could accept a certain level of staged cultural events, as opposed to foreign tourists who were worried about the lack of authenticity.

Overtourism and commodification also lead to a competition between different sites over claims of authenticity. For example, Arlt and Hu, when looking at Ganzi prefecture in Sichuan Province found "competing claims as to being the origin of 'authentic' Xuanzi, a kind of local music, or for being the 'authentic' holy mountain" (Arlt and Hu 2009, p. 174). Increased tourism caused "a new wave of production of local history and culture, often including factual misconstruction, to gain a unique market position while creating manufactured authenticities of Shangri-La in the market" (Arlt and Hu 2009, p. 174).

In researching Naxi guesthouses in Lijiang in 2001, Wang found that "the biggest group of respondents claimed that seeking an 'authentic' Naxi cultural experience was their primary reason for choosing a homestay in Lijiang" (Wang 2007, p. 792). However, the guesthouse owners themselves did not view their guest houses as 'authentic' due to the modifications they had to do to convert their homes into proper guesthouses, including "flush toilets, bathtubs, TV sets, and telephones" and, breaking with Naxi cultural traditions, adding windows to the guest rooms, as well as changing the food they cooked and the language they spoke (Wang 2007, p. 793). Wang points out that, despite the 'staged' nature of the Naxi homestays, "its authenticity can still be perceived and even enjoyed by the guests" (ibid: 795), thus going against the idea of objective authenticity as being the goal of such touristic activities. This is labelled as 'customized authenticity,' which "both originates in and orients tourist demands, behaviors, perceptions, and imaginings toward the authenticity of the toured object," part of the "age of consumerism in which all industries try to customize their products to best meet consumers' demands" (Wang 2007, p. 797). In their case, this co-construction of authenticity by the hosts and the guests creates "a variety of customized authenticities . . . which closely fits the tourist taste for decentralized and non-standardized products" (ibid: 798).

Wang's (2007) research was followed up by Shi *et al.* (2020), who also looked at Naxi guesthouses. They found additional aspects in their surveys, such as that the object-related authenticity ("environment and folk customs of the guesthouse") does not contribute to the tourists' "sense of being at home," likely due to "exotic and unfamiliar feeling[s]" caused by the new environment, and that "tourists' perception of object-related authenticity has a positive effect on tourists' perceptions of existential authenticity" (Shi *et al.* 2020, p. 1148).

Others have noted that Chinese and other 'eastern' conceptions of 'authenticity' vary greatly from Western perspectives. Li and Sofield argue that for Chinese tourists

> a newly engraved inscription may have an authenticity similar to a much older inscription because they 'see' the continuity in an age-old process that should not be 'museumized' according to some western notion of separating the past from the present.
>
> (Li and Sofield 2009, p. 166)

As can be seen, the majority of research on authenticity is from ethnic minority tourism. There are plenty of other sites for tourism in China that do not rely on minority culture to attract tourists, and it is not only minority culture that can be represented inauthentically.

Rationale

To better explore some of the issues in tourism authenticity in China, this study will examine six sites which deal with touristic authenticity in three ways: preserving, miniaturizing, and replicating. Preserving is, in many ways, the act of not destroying a traditional cultural heritage site and instead managing it in such a way that it becomes dependent on tourism for its survival. Miniaturizing can take the forms of dioramas or models or, in extreme cases, entire theme parks entirely consisting of miniaturized versions of tourist sites. Replicating involves the recreation, from scratch, of unique buildings, cityscapes, and other features from faraway lands.

We will first introduce the categorization of the six tourist sites to give a better overview, focusing on defining what type of site they are, how they fulfil tourists' needs, their relationship (or lack thereof) with locals, and how one has to cross a boundary to enter them.

Type of Sites

We will distinguish the sites using the criteria provided by du Cros and McKercher (2015, p. 109). Different tourist attractions have different "demand generation potential," with more dominant ones having a high sense of "obligation" for tourists to visit, while moving to the other end of the spectrum causes attractions to be "increasingly discretionary" (du Cros and McKercher 2015, p. 109). Second is the market orientation of the sites, in that the "more mainstream or mass the market being drawn to the attraction is, the easier the product must be to consume" especially as "Mainstream tourists are usually motivated by pleasure or escape reasons" and "enjoyable experiences that do not tax them mentally or ideologically" (du Cros and McKercher 2015, p. 115). Third is the nature of all of the sites as being purpose-built tourist attractions, one theme being "tourismification of the extant yet previously undeveloped heritage assets" and the other the "building of purpose-built cultural or heritage theme parks" (du Cros and McKercher 2015, p. 201). Du Cros and McKercher (2015, pp. 201–202) also argue that "purpose-built theme parks" with a "heritage flavor" are usually built by the private sector with a profit motive, and thus "provide a better quality" while being "clearly less authentic" than "extant facilities."

These sites also have a unique, ambiguous relationship to the notion of cultural tourism in general. Du Cros and McKercher define cultural tourism

Table 1.2 Types of Sites

	Name	*Demand Generation Potential*	*Market Orientation*	*Style*	*Theme*
Preservation	Huitong Village	Low	Local	Tourisimified extant asset	Pre-modern China
	Mt. Yunji	Low	Local	Purpose-built	Ancient China
Miniaturization	Window of the World	High	National/ international	Purpose-built	International
	Splendid China	High	National/ international	Purpose-built	Universalized China
Replication	Hallstatt Huizhou	Mid	Local/ provincial	Purpose-built	General European
	Venetian Macau	High	International	Purpose-built	Specific Italianate European

as "representing a product class of experiences and activities that embodies a destination's cultural heritage assets" (du Cros and McKercher 2015, p. 9). Yet we would like to problematize this distinction. What if the 'product class of experiences and activities' are from outside the destination's culture but created by the local culture, such as with theme parks, themed malls, and themed casinos? What 'cultural heritage assets' do Las Vegas or Macau casinos have that represents what might be called 'authentic local culture'? Can we not say that themed malls and casinos are the local culture of these locations? One travels to the Venetian not because they want to go to a mall or casino, but due to the theme, and such theming of a mall/casino is an authentic cultural practice of that location done better there than at other locations.

For theme parks featuring miniature replications of attractions from around the world, such as the various Legoland parks or, in our case, Window of the World and Splendid China, the attraction has almost no relationship to any 'local' culture. Certainly, Splendid China features miniatures of temples, palaces, and other buildings and natural wonders from around China and is made by Chinese people in China, but it is in Shenzhen which is a notoriously *new* city which was built on the site of a fishing village only due to its proximity to the border with Hong Kong. There are attractions in Shenzhen about Shenzhen's history, such as the Huaqiangbei Museum detailing the history of their tech industry, and exhibitions about the move from copy tech coming from Hong Kong to the modern innovative tech sector.

But Window of the World and Splendid China are tourist sites about tourist sites. Indeed, they are more like permanent international or national expos, which are "a kind of micro-version of international tourism" (Urry and Larson 2011, p. 133). The whole purpose of these sites is to allow visitors "to experience and gaze upon different signs" from around the world by "conveniently [bringing them] together in one location" (Urry and Larson 2011, p. 133).

National Cultural Assets "symbolize a society's shared recollections" and "represent much about how it expresses its identity through valorization of durable national icons that reflect national pride" (du Cros and McKercher 2015, p. 28). Tourists from, in our case, China, "may feel a sense of pilgrimage by visiting these places and paying homage to national symbols that represent their shared identity," yet the World Heritage Attractions "draw large numbers of tourists that invoke feelings of awe" but they "probably do not invoke feelings of deep personal attachment" (du Cros and McKercher 2015, p. 28). They argue that the 'personal impact' felt by visiting attractions depends on how closely they are connected to a locality, "direct and highly personal at the neighbourhood or community level," while being "indirect and more philosophical at the national or international level" (du Cros and McKercher 2015, p. 28)

However, du Cros and McKercher are talking about the, for lack of a better word, 'authentic' assets and attractions, the Great Wall or the Eiffel Tower itself. What level of 'deep feelings' or 'sense of pilgrimage' could emerge from visiting miniature replicas of such attractions? You cannot tell friends and family that you have visited the Pyramids and had a transcendent experience due to their vast scale and incomprehensible age, only that it was cool to see a replica of them and to criticize or praise the attempt at mimicry after taking a photo.

Fulfilling Needs

du Cros and McKercher argue that cultural tourism "sells dreams" and the respective tourists participate in order "to have an inner need satisfied, regardless of whether the person is seeking a deep or shallow experience" (2015, pp. 156–158). They thus advise that tourism developers first understand "what the market wants" and then somehow devise "goods and services that satisfy those wants" (du Cros and McKercher 2015, pp. 156–158).

Window of the World and Splendid China arguably 'fill the need' to travel around the world and China, respectively, at a lesser cost and with assumed lower fidelity. Hallstatt Huizhou and Venetian Macau 'fill the need' to travel to idyllic foreign scenery, similarly more cost-effectively and with lower expectations for authenticity, although higher than a miniature theme park. As with other themed casinos, Venetian Macau was developed due to the success of the Venetian Las Vegas, with the success of the latter validating the creation of the former. Mt Yunji and Huitong Village 'fill the need' to travel back to a traditional and historical version of China. Mt Yunji was developed to create a reconstructed traditional village for preservation means with tourism as an ancillary concern, while Huitong Village's development into a tourist attraction was part of national and local preservation efforts.

Locals

Their relationship with the locals is also quite unique. Much of the concerns in tourism research and cultural preservation efforts are related to the impact that it has on the locals, ensuring that their ways of life are not disrupted too much, they have some measure of control over how their culture is commodified, and they receive appropriate compensation. Boorstin (1961) argues this is the perfect example of how our lives are overwhelmed by contrived experiences, and tourists have become more passive onlookers who are separated from the local environment. Resorts and themed malls, "enclavic spaces stimulating primarily the visual sense," are analytically different from spaces where tourists and locals co-mingle (Urry and Larson 2011, p. 154)

This is often conceptualized as the different 'stages' on which tourists and locals interact. MacCannel (1973) borrows this concept from Goffman (1959), in that cultures present themselves in a different way to guests via the front stage while maintaining their own culture and community in the backstage inaccessible to visitors and tourists. MacCannel also shows how tourist sites often create 'fake' backstages, areas that look like where the locals actually live their day-to-day life but are still commodified cultural assets themselves. While this will be discussed in greater detail in the next chapter, it is enough to note for now that these chosen sites lack this traditional division between back and front, largely because all the sites, other than Huitong Village, lack locals.

For the other sites, there is no backstage as there are no locals. The only place we might define as a backstage would be the employees' breakrooms, and there seems to be little interest in viewing lockers and tables stacked with used Tupperware. They exist as pure signs of only the front stage. In Austrian Hallstatt and Venetian Venice, all that is left is the fake backstages and front stages. Tourism itself led to the destruction of the backstage area of these and other overtouristed sites.

For our study, only Huitong Village has a local population. Yet they are not 'ethnic' in the broad sense of the term, not an ethnic minority group or special class of people with a unique way of life. Tourists going to Huitong only consume a very generic early twentieth-century Lingnan-style village life. This is slowly disappearing across China, and of course other developing countries around the world, due to the massive urbanization campaign, and definitely need to be preserved. At the same, tourists do not go to Huitong to consume the Huitong villagers' way of life because the villagers there do not live their life very differently than the tourists do.

This begs an interesting question. The value of cultural assets "comes from its meaning to a community or its existence value" and "not from its revenue-generating potential" (McKercher and du Cros 2005, p. 46). But what if such an asset has no community to give it meaning, its existence only to generate revenue?

Boundary Crossing

Of course, there must be a difference between 'travel' and 'tourism' as "all travel involves some cultural element" because we inevitably move from "a comfortable home culture" to "a somewhat alien culture," and this basic element is true if it is to a further away, more foreign destination or "only to a nearby domestic destination" (du Cros and McKercher 2015, p. 4). One element these sites have in common with other tourism sites is that to gain access one has to cross into another kind of space, what van den Berghe (1980, p. 377) terms "a conscious crossing of ethnic boundaries" or what Urry and Larson call a "liminal zone" between "the familiar and the faraway" (Urry and Larson 2011, p. 13). They all feature "the central exploitable element" of tourism, "*exoticism*" in that "the tourist comes to see and experience something [they] cannot duplicate at home" such as "a different climate, landscape, flora and fauna, or different cultures, past and present" (van den Berghe 1980, p. 377).

The consuming difference is the main objective of cultural tourists, and ensuring there is something 'different' to consume is the main goal of tourism operators. Local tourist attractions and sites might have little difference between their own culture and aesthetics than the surrounding area, yet they can make themselves special and exotic by deploying exotic signs to better differentiate themselves.

'Ethnic' restaurants routinely do so by giving signs of the cuisine's culture and/or country through stereotypical decorations, such as flags, statues, shrines, photos of celebrities, the choice of colours, and plastic versions of typical foods. Consider a typical Italian restaurant anywhere in the world: it *needs* to be decorated with signs of 'Italian restaurant,' such as Italian flags, bundles of garlic hanging from the ceiling, white- and red-patterned tablecloths, miniature statues of the Italian Chef, photos of famous places like the Coliseum and Leaning Tower of Pisa, cans of tomato paste, and so on. To enter an Italian restaurant with no signs of an Italian Restaurant would be very disturbing as crossing that boundary from the real world to Italian Restaurant is part of the experience. At the same time, what an authentic Italian Restaurant looks like is entirely irrelevant. There is a code of Italian Restaurant that needs to be adhered to globally, and the code even operates in Italy itself where tourist-oriented restaurants have changed their signs to fit the international standard of Italian Restaurant. The same goes for other international cuisines. Thai or Chinese or Japanese restaurants around the world offer nearly identical menus and decorations because that is the boundary we must cross to enter that other culture and successfully enjoy that other cuisine.

To enter all six sites under study here, we have to cross a boundary, although it varies greatly for ease of access via transportation, entry price, and the aesthetic features tourists come across.

Mt Yunji is located at the top of a hill and thus requires a windy drive up a steep road through the forest for over 30 minutes. You enter through a traditional Chinese archway, past the storage area in the front will piles of wood and brick lying around, the re-claimed materials not yet re-assembled. The parking is limited, but once you turn to the village itself, you are met with a giant water wheel next to a large stone archway leading to the main village.

Huitong Village is not centrally located in Zhuhai city proper, but it is a convenient drive and features plentiful parking and is free to enter. Other than the nearby university, it is not in walkable distance to other communities in the area as most of the former farmland has been used as development for the university, new high-rise housing, and light industry factories. From the parking lot, one enters by walking past the tourist centre and over two small bridges themselves listed as intangible cultural heritage assets. As with Mt Yunji you are met with, on the right side, a pleasant small lake surrounded by trees, and, on the left, the Mo Family Ancestral Hall.

For Window of the World and Splendid China, the journey there is quite convenient as it is in the middle of the city with quick access by subway and public transportation, although parking is quite limited. The entry is very much like a theme park, needing the purchase of a ticket. After the main gate, you are confronted by a confusing assemblage of architectural signs from around the world: free-standing columns and statues with varying styles (Chinese, Roman, Greek, Hindu, Assyrian, etc.) lined up in a semi-circle around a round stage whose roof resembles a map of the Northern Hemisphere of the earth. It is far from subtle, to say the least.

Venetian Macau is free to enter, although it is virtually an island, as with most of the casinos in the Cotai area of Macau, being accessible by taxi, shuttle, or car, and definitely inaccessible by walking. You first have to enter via the hotel or casino part of the complex and then walk for 15 to 20 minutes to get to the actual Grand Canal area. The boundary crossing in fact first occurs when approaching the complex itself from the outside, as the external decorations are an assemblage of buildings and bridges from Venice. For example, a Ponte di Rialto replica acts as a 'bridge' crossing the street between an entrance and a massive replica of St. Mark's Campanile, with the outside of the main building covered in a façade resembling the Piazza San Marco and other generic Venetian-style buildings in the back. Entering the casino or hotel, you are confronted by more glitzy aesthetics, white columns with gold trim, faux marble, and recreations of famous paintings on the ceiling.

Hallstatt Huizhou is in a suburb of Huizhou and requires a long drive, a ticket for entry, and a shuttle to bring you from the parking to the main gate. Once you disembark from the shuttle, you have to cross a non-descript bridge and can immediately see the striking replica of the Hallstatt Church on the man-made lake. However, the view is confusing as all the trees and plants are local tropical variants, such as palm trees and banyan trees, and the artificial lake is a muddy brown.

The aforementioned description is not to criticize the lack of authenticity of the sites but instead to describe how their boundaries act to give signs to the visitors that they are, indeed, crossing a boundary.

Can we say that the European versions of Hallstatt and Venice are more authentic than the Chinese versions? That they are the 'originals' and only the Chinese ones should be called 'versions'? The Chinese versions do not have a 'local' population that a tourist would visit, yet do the European versions? Both have been markedly changed by tourism to the point that they are nearly bereft of a "local" population, with Venetian locals diminishing year by year. The locals (shopkeepers, waitstaff, guards) in Chinese Hallstatt are "local" in that they are from the surrounding area, or perhaps are migrant workers from further afield. The locals in the Venetian, by contrast, are from around the world, most being Macanese or Chinese Mainlanders, but with a high proportion of Filipino and European shopkeepers, waiters, hotel staff, performers, etc. In the European versions, the remaining locals are similarly shopkeepers, waiters, and hotel staff from the local area. Are they more authentic because the locals are culturally closer to the culture whose signs are being consumed by the tourists? Would Chinese Hallstatt be "more authentic" if it brought in several chefs from Austria to cook Hallstatt cuisine instead of providing typical Chinese tourist cuisine? Venetian Macau features a wide range of mid-to-high-cost restaurants and cuisines from all around the world, very little of its authentic Venetian food, yet also importing Venetian chefs or focusing on Italian food, for example, would not help due to its more international and high-class nature.

Methodology

Chinese language studies about authenticity in Chinese tourist sites tend to fall along three lines, either review articles, quantitative surveys, or a smaller amount of qualitative examinations. Zhu and Lu (2005) argue that international studies on cultural tourism mainly focus on heritage site tourism, in terms of sustainable development, influence of heritage tourism, development of heritage tourism, values of heritage tourism, and so forth, while domestic studies on cultural tourism mainly focus on sustainable development issues.

Review articles tend to be purely theoretical but not necessarily aimed at developing *new* theories or pushing existing theories forward, being more instrumental in nature. Zhou *et al.* (2007) theorize about different concepts of authenticity to get "a better understanding of tourism authenticity so as to better instruct the development of tourism resources" (Zhou *et al.* 2007, p. 46). Dong *et al.* (2017) performed a similar review with updated material but still do not offer any theoretical innovation.

The majority of studies do rely on quantitative studies based on surveys of tourists' perceptions. This includes Chen and Chen (2021), Chao and Wang (2021), Gao and Zheng 2010), Chen and Zhao (2021), Jin *et al.* (2022), Wang and Wu (2013), Wang and Wu (2013), Zhou and Yu (2004), Shi *et al.* (2020), and Yang and Wall (2010). They are mostly instrumental in nature, concerning tourists feeling about authenticity with the conclusion being advice about how to improve or protect authenticity at the various tourist sites. Other studies are more innovative; as mentioned earlier, Wang and Chen (2020) analysed the soundscape of the tourist site. Tian (2005) used a survey combined with fieldwork, observation, and interviews.

Internationally, a more diverse array of methods have been deployed to examine authenticity in tourism, ranging from surveys of tourists (i.e. Chhabra *et al.* 2003; Pocock 1992; Wang and Wu 2013; Yang and Wall 2010), to a semiotic or aesthetic analysis, to a more integrated ethnographic approach (i.e. Cohen 1972; Hom 2010; van den Berghe 1980), or an even more complicated combination of all of the above (i.e. Bruner 1994; Walby and Piché 2015). This depends, it seems, on the perspective taken on where authenticity lies; with the cultural artefacts and practices and the built environment or with the experiences and perspectives of the tourists themselves.

As Olsen notes, "If people's experience of being tourists is what keeps them away from what they regard as authentic experiences," then an analysis "has to pay attention to how people are situated in a social context when they label experiences authentic or not" (Olsen 2002, p. 161). Yang and Wall (2010) conducted extensive quantitative surveys in Xishuangbanna, Yunnan, finding that Chinese tourists could accept a certain level of staged cultural events, as opposed to foreign tourists who were worried about the lack of authenticity. Chhabra *et al.* (2003) did a quantitative survey of attendees of a Scottish cultural heritage festival. Yet they did not perform an analysis of the aesthetics, cultural forms, and simulacra present at the tourist site.

Hom (2010) engages with "the tenets of anthropological participant-observation and ethnographic documentation" (Hom 2010, p. 379). Hom' study includes an extensive description of the semiotics of the theme parks and efforts made to make the site resemble Venice, in other words their efforts to produce signs of authenticity. Walby and Piché, by contrast, use a combination of data from "photographs and videos, field notes from guided tours" and participant-observation of and "semi-structured interviews with museum operators and (un)paid workers" (Walby and Piché 2015 235). While these studies gathered a lot of aesthetic and contextual data, neither gathered data from tourists themselves, however. Sakwit (2021), on the other hand, included aesthetic analysis with interviews of both tourists and tourism workers.

Surveys or interviews with tourists themselves which explore their perceptions of feelings on authenticity can only reveal a part of the picture, as will be explained further in the next section.

Methods

This study is squarely qualitative in nature. It combines short interviews, aesthetic analysis, and examination of online reviews to create a broader picture and capture multiple perspectives on authenticity.

First are interviews conducted on the sites. Unfortunately, due to the COVID-19 pandemic, interviews were only able to be conducted on four sites. Interviews were conducted on-site. Statistical data about the interviewees, such as gender and age, were not gathered as the sample size was too small for these kinds of variables to be measured in any meaningful way. Instead, the variables are limited to the specific sites visited and the origin of the interviewees. We determined three categories, locals who reside in the city where the site is, domestic tourists who travelled from outside the immediate locality for the purpose of tourism, and foreign tourists. Respondents were interviewed at each site until saturation was reached.

The participants were asked four open questions, the first two to establish where they were from, what kind of tourist they were, and the other two to enquire about their motivations for visiting the site and their feelings about the authenticity of the site (i.e. "What do you think about the authenticity of [site name]?"). This was done to allow the interviewees to be able to frame answers in their own words and to allow for greater time to get more detailed explanations of their reasons. The questions were limited in number in order to ensure they completed the interview and, as mentioned, to allow more detailed answers. Due to travel restrictions during the pandemic, we were not able to travel to all six tourist sites to conduct interviews with tourists, however.

Second is the aesthetic analysis of the signs of authenticity generated by the sites. While this description may sound a bit obtuse, it is a fair description of what poststructuralist research can do as we researchers do not have some privileged position whereby we can judge if something is authentic or not. We can look at the signs present in the tourist sites, put there purposefully by the creators and operators of the tourist site.

Third is an analysis of reviews of the sites on travel websites and apps, cTrip for Chinese-language reviews and TripAdvisor for English-language ones. The number of reviews varied a lot from each site; therefore, data collection was stopped when we felt we had reached saturation with the variety of ways in which reviews discussed authenticity. More detail will be provided in the analysis part of each chapter in regard to this.

Outline

The next chapter will first explore the effects of commodification on tourism, including the implications of the transformation of tangible and intangible cultural heritage assets into products. We will then adapt the epistemological theoretical framework from Hearns-Branaman (2011, 2016) to research on tourism and authenticity. We will then introduce Hyperrealism and show how it has been explored in tourism literature before developing the concept of pseudo-authenticity. Three analytical categories will be elucidated. The remaining three chapters will explore each category of tourist site; preservation, miniaturization, and replication.

2 Commodification and Epistemology

In this chapter, we will further elaborate on the epistemological framework we will use to examine these six tourist sites. We will first examine the effects of commodification and mass tourism on cultural heritage assets as they are transformed into consumable products. We will then examine three epistemological theories derived from the theoretical framework of Hearns-Branaman (2011, 2016), Realism, Pragmatism, and Hyperrealism, and relate them to the existing epistemological debates in the tourism literature, thereby developing the theory of pseudo-authenticity.

Finally, we will create the three analytical categories used to analyse the data. The first category concerns the influence of the media on tourism, that media give us a set of presumptions about tourist sites, influences how we decode the signs of the sites, and then how we re-encode the signs via photography. The transformation of cultural assets into products leads to two outcomes, the enjoyment of the fakery by tourists and reliance on facades to provide signs for them to consume.

Commodification of Tourism

The impact of capitalism and commodification on culture has been a major concern of research over the last century. To get into a thorough examination of the concerns is out of the scope of this chapter and this book as a whole. It can best be surmised by observations of Kracauer over 90 years ago: "Community and personality perish when what is demanded is calculability" (Kracauer 1927, p. 78). The fight in the capitalist era has thus been to create a balance to preserve community, personality, culture, and creativity while at the same time creating a profit so that cultural can continue to survive through the culture industries.

Kracauer continues: "Since the principle of the capitalist production process does not arise purely out of nature, it must destroy the natural organisms that it regards either as means or as a resistance" (Kracauer 1927, p. 78). In other words, the concern is that the capitalist processes will either destroy 'natural' human activity or co-opt it, commodifying it without regard to its

DOI: 10.4324/9781003291817-2

'natural' intentions. This goes for all cultural activities, from dance to music to art to architecture. And tourism, of course, as it consists of cultural assets that have been transformed into products that are put on display and put on sale to tourists.

Boorstin expressed his concerns about this process as well, arguing that tourist attractions are "of little significance for the inward life of a people, but wonderfully salable as a tourist commodity" (Boorstin 1961, p. 103). Even tourist sites based on natural phenomena, Boorstin's example being the geysers of Yellowstone National Park, are popular and famous because the geysers "erupt and boil on schedule" and are thus "closest to the artificial 'regular' tourist performances" that we have become used to, and thus are "Nature imitating the pseudo-event" (Boorstin 1961, p. 111). Geysers with irregular eruption cycles are harder to become consistent tourist attractions because they cannot be commodified easily. Whale watching, for example, would not be possible without advanced technology, as seasonal and whale migration paths are not easily predictable. Tourist operators have to take great effort in tracking them in order to increase the chances their passengers will see whales, thus turning these natural phenomena into a predictable and commodifiable experience.

Boorstin posits that "the traveler used to go about the world to encounter the natives"; however, with the advent of mass tourism this is no longer possible (Boorstin 1961, pp. 91–92). The use of travel agencies, as discussed earlier, helps "to prevent this encounter" because their goal is to "devis[e] efficient new ways of insulating the tourist from the travel world" (Boorstin 1961, pp. 91–92). This causes increased isolation of the tourist from the local culture: "The tourist who arrives at his destination, where tourist facilities have been 'improved,' remains almost as insulated as he was en route. Today the ideal tourist hotel abroad is as much as possible like the best accommodations back home" (Boorstin 1961, p. 97). This standardization of tourism facilities is increasingly global and an especially a feature of the international hotel chains which rely on tourists anticipating their experience will be nearly identical no matter where in the world they travel.

Cohen (1988) makes a similar case, that "commoditization allegedly changes the meaning of cultural products and of human relations, making them eventually meaningless" (Cohen 1988, p. 372). This is a fair criticism, as the consumption of rituals and artefacts does have a meaning to tourists, however not the original meaning they had pre-tourism; the tourists are consuming signs of the pre-touristic rituals and artefacts in a self-referential meaning-making cycle. The meaning changes to being about consumption itself and the touristic experience, not the actual lived lives of the culture that tourists are visiting. In the end, " 'colorful' local costumes and customs, rituals and feasts, and folk and ethnic arts become touristic services or commodities, as they come to be performed or produced for touristic consumption" (Cohen 1988, p. 372), that is, as opposed to being performed for community-based rituals.

Put in terms of more typical tourism research, "The more mainstream or mass the market being drawn to the attraction is, the easier the product must be to consume" (du Cros and McKercher 2015, p. 115). Just as with other consumer goods and mass media products, reaching the lowest common denominator in the market requires dumbing down, simplifying, and standardizing a product. There is also always space for a niche or specialized market to reach smaller consumer subsets and elites, like with the Grand Tour mentioned in the last chapter, such as private luxury yacht cruises, personal tours, or exclusive restaurants. Yet the mass market is where the focus of the industry lies, and most tourist sites and experiences have been adapted to serve the masses. Still, du Cros and McKercher (2015, p. 113) make an important point:

> On the one hand, providing experiences that require greater effort to consume may result in lower visitation, which could affect the commercial viability of a product. On the other hand, making the product simple to consume may result in higher visitation, but at cost to the quality of the message being sent.

Developing tourism products requires careful planning because you need a balance between the specific elements that will draw the specific tourist market developers are after while being mindful of the expense of getting to the destination. In other words, the planners must "create a sufficiently satisfying experience that is unique, exciting, and offers 'one of a kind' encounters that appeal to the target market to warrant the cost associated with reaching the attraction or destination" (du Cros and McKercher 2015, p. 153). If the site is generic but has a popular theme which can reach a wider market segment and is easily accessible, think of theme parks like Disneyland or Disneyworld, then the project can be successful.

If the theme is very specific, the target market smaller, and is located in an inconvenient place, then you have to temper your expectations for the number of visitors and long-term viability. At the same time, for this type of site, investment can be made in increasing accessibility, creating a wider variety of attractions and broadening the potential market. Angkor Wat in Siem Reap, Cambodia, is a good example of this. It is a very unique and part of a well-preserved temple complex hundreds of years old in the middle of the jungle in an economically impoverished country which faced devastating internal conflict not 30 years ago. Early foreign visitors were explorers, historians, and archaeologists in the mid-1800s interested in the temple for scientific reasons. Yet starting in the 1990s with the development of transportation infrastructure in the form of an airport with good regional connections, as well as good roads to the temples, the training of tour guides and creation of tour packages, the growth in restaurants, cafes, hotels, and other amenities, the Angkor Wat has become one of the top tourist destinations in the world. The short-term consequence is very positive for the local and national economy, yet in the long term, the site faces overtourism which could lead to the temple being permanently damaged. Sustainable development models thus need to be created in order to protect the site, as discussed in the previous chapter.

While the sustainability of tangible cultural products is an important issue, for our purposes we will emphasize more on the major side effects of unsustainable cultural tourism development and "cultural commodification" being the "loss of authenticity" (du Cros and McKercher (2015, p. 37). For example, research has found "those who come to seek the authenticity of being close to nature may turn to other places after their first visitation because of the park's loss of naturalness and increased commercialization" (Zhong *et al.* 2009, p. 65).

Yet the question remains, what exactly is authenticity? If we can 'lose' authenticity through commodification how does that process happen? This will be explored in greater detail in the next section, focusing primarily on the effects of turning cultural assets into tourism products.

Cultural Heritage Assets and Products

> The sight-seeing items [i.e. assets] which can be confidently guaranteed and conveniently and quickly delivered to tourists on arrival have these merchandisable qualities precisely because they are not native expressions of the country.
>
> (Boorstin 1961, p. 108)

Heritage tourism is the result of demand from tourists "to directly experience and consume diverse past and present cultural landscapes, performances, food, handicrafts, and participatory activities" (Chhabra *et al.* 2003, p. 703). Yet these activities cannot be experienced directly by tourists as such participatory activities are tied to a community in which the tourist is inherently an outsider. Furthermore, tangible assets are typically not made with the intention of being visited by 1) masses of people who are 2) outsiders. Thus, the whole series of tangible and intangible cultural heritage assets need to be transformed into something else that tourists can consume.

The best way to describe this transformation, from traveller to tourist, from nature to capital, from tangible or intangible culture to something consumable, is that cultural tourism takes a set of "cultural heritage *assets* and transforms them into *products* that can be consumed by tourists" (McKercher and du Cros 2005, pp. 211–212, emphasis added). It is important to make a distinction between "a cultural asset/item" and "a cultural tourism product" as the former is "uncommodified or raw" while the latter "has been transformed or commodified specifically for tourism consumption" (du Cros and McKercher 2015, p. 7). A tourism product is traditionally defined as "anything that can be offered to a market for attention, acquisition, use or consumption that might satisfy and need or want" (Kotler and Turner 1989, p. 435).

Changing a cultural asset into a tourist product always requires "some level of modification, commodification, and standardization of the asset," processes that make "abstract experiences concrete" (McKercher and du Cros 2002, p. 115). Cultural assets should be "identified, performed, safeguarded, handed down, and/or conserved for their intrinsic values or significance to a community rather than for their extrinsic use values as tourism attractions" (du Cros and McKercher 2015, p. 6), yet this ethical need is always in conflict with the needs of tourism to provide concrete products for them to consume.

For example, historical buildings and sites tend to go through expensive renovations and other kinds of work after their original purpose is finished in order to make them acceptable tourist sites (Staples 1995). This includes the creation of transportation infrastructure, from airports to trains to busses on the larger scale, and safe walkways with guardrails, escalators or elevators, and maps and signs on the smaller scale. It also can include the installation of 'modern conveniences,' such as toilets and baby changing stations, Wi-Fi and phone charging stations, and lighting, all which of might not have existed at an appropriate scale to meet the needs of tourists.

Examples of this have been discussed throughout tourism literature. Cohen notes that " 'colorful' local costumes and customs, rituals and feasts, and folk and ethnic arts become touristic services or commodities, as they come to be performed or produced for touristic consumption" (Cohen 1988, p. 372). More recently, Sakwit shows how the Damnoen Saduak Floating Market in Thailand has "changed in accordance with the needs of tourism" including aspects like "its purpose, products, [and] pattern of trading," all "in order to target tourist arrivals and meet demand" (Sakwit 2021, p. 5).

Studies such as Zhou and Yu (2004) found that all respondents found that the inclusion of tourism-related facilities in a natural landscape decreases the quality of the aesthetic value, in this case of a park including a unique landscape of quartz stone. Zhang and Lee (2020) examine authenticity in tourism products from the perspective of 'alienation,' in fact arguing that "alienation might be more applicable than authenticity" when looking at how intangible cultural heritage products are created (ibid: 3). That is to say, the move between the intangible asset of, in their case, choral music and the tourism product creates alienation between the local producers and the touristic version of their choral music.

Bruner gives an excellent extended analysis of this for the New Salem historical site, noting that "there are many conscious compromises to authenticity," and while "some are necessary for the creation of longevity of the site," the others are mostly "designed to make the visitors' experience more enjoyable" (Bruner 1994, p. 401). He, however, waves away concerns about the effect of the change from assets to products as a "compromise" which is simply some of "the little white lies of historical reconstruction" as the function to "make the reconstructed New Salem better than the original, at least for contemporary tourists" (Bruner 1994, p. 401). These include gutters, fences and gates, modern restrooms, drinking fountains, benches, paved roads, heaters, wheelchair ramps, a mowed lawn, and the lack of smaller, temporary structures common at that time (ibid: 401–402). The houses on the site are made to look weathered; although as Bruner points out, the original village only lasted for 10 years, not long enough to be naturally weathered, and this is done to be "more credible to visitors" while being "a less accurate reproduction of the 1830s" (ibid: 402). Bruner defends these 'little white lies' because the role of the site is to be "more believable to 1990s tourists" who expect "a more suburban version of history" (Bruner 1994, p. 402).

This description is, in fact, emblematic of poststructuralist views of authenticity in tourism; the site is made to be better than the original, to be more real than real through the use of signs of history, ones that point to what modern people would expect from history. Typically, however, these changes are viewed as being either positive as they allow for new cultural forms to emerge, or negative, as they corrupt the original culture. As early as the 1980s, van den Berghe pointed out this positive potential. "In response to the ethnic tourist's demand for exoticism and authenticity, ethnic consciousness of the natives can be heightened, and markers of ethnic distinctiveness emphasized," which can "lead to cultural revivalism as when art forms, dances and ceremonies are created or recreated for tourist consumption," yet such "cultural creations or recreations" can "lead to entirely new cultural forms that are only pseudo-traditional" (van den Berghe (1980, pp. 389–390).

Tourism is achieved through the transformation of both tangible and intangible cultural assets into cultural products which can be consumed tangibly and intangibly. This transformation greatly problematizes any notions of 'authenticity' as originally conceived, that is, 'objective authenticity' whereby the precise origins and originality of a cultural asset are the whole point. An authentic cartouche or statue, a tangible Egyptian cultural asset, robbed from the tombs of Egypt can be defined as being objectively authentic through a scientific process; a 'replica' cartouche or statue, on the other hand, cannot be sold as an objectively authentic product because the signs of the object have been redeployed into an inauthentic cultural product and thus lacks origins and originality. Similarly, the authentic experience of staying in a Mongolian yurt or Naxi house, as the locals would do in their daily life, or praying at a temple or shrine or wearing unique local clothing cannot, by definition, be objectively authentic. The yurt or other domicile, a cultural asset with both tangible and intangible aspects, needs to be transformed into a tourism product which gives signs of an authentic experience; the tourist feigns a prayer or temporarily wears the unique local clothing, all while their travelmates take photos, to consume signs of authentic culture.

This also begs the question: what if there was no 'raw' asset to be transformed and instead the product itself was the 'original' asset? There is a difference between commodifying Italian Venice for tourism and creating a Las Vegan/Macanese Venice from scratch already to be consumed. No transformation or commodification has taken place because the site is already commodified. The process is to transform a cultural asset into a product, yet these are already cultural products. This begs the question: What happens when you transform a cultural product into another cultural product?

To further explore the implications of this transformation, we now need to turn to an examination of the epistemological theories that help us better define what we actually mean when we say 'authentic.' Instead of going through the normal review of different definitions and categorizations of authenticity, we will instead use the epistemological schemas as developed by Hearns-Branaman (2011, 2016) and relate them to the existing tourism literature.

Realism

> [R]eality is but a concept, or a principle, and by reality I mean the whole system of values connected with this principle. The Real as such implies an origin, an end, a past and a future, a chain of causes and effects, continuity and rationality. No real without these elements, without an objective configuration of discourse. And its disappearing is the dislocation of the whole constellation.
>
> (Baudrillard 2000, p. 63)

The first epistemological theory we will look at is Realism. Realism is "the theory that our thoughts and understanding of the world have a direct relationship with the way the world exists outside of our minds" (Hearns-Branaman 2016, p. 25). Realists "have to constitute truth as correspondence to reality" and "must also argue that there are procedures of justification of belief which are natural and not merely local" (Rorty 1991, p. 22). As Russell puts it, "a belief is true when there is a corresponding fact, and is false when there is no corresponding fact" (Russell 1912, p. 129).

This 'correspondence' theory of truth "comes from the Platonic tradition of thought" instead of "theological or authoritarian epistemology" in which "Truth was decreed not discovered" (Hearns-Branaman 2016, p. 27). It emerged during the Enlightenment with the "rediscovery of Greek Philosophy," and the goal was "to figure out the best way to have our knowledge correspond to an external Reality" (Hearns-Branaman 2016, p. 27). The continental and Anglophone traditions did diverge, with those like Kant advocating for the explorations of 'conceptual schemes' to "better understand the limitations of sensory input to lets us achieve a better view and hence understanding of the world" (Hearns-Branaman 2016, p. 27). Meanwhile, while those like Locke and Hume were more positivists, viewing "sensory experience and empirical evidence as what is needed for our minds to better reflect Reality" (Hearns-Branaman 2016, p. 27). This changed in the twentieth century with a focus on language in that "language has replaced mind as that which, supposedly, stands over and against 'reality'" (Rorty 1991, p. 2), at least for philosophers, linguists, and humanities scholars.

For historians, especially those involved in studying artefacts, this evolved into an emphasis on finding ways to scientifically validate the provenance and authenticity of the objects of their research. Early concerns about authenticity were confined mostly to the provenance of certain artefacts, paintings, sculptures, and the like, in that they were not counterfeit and had been identified (authorship, age, etc.) properly. As Trilling (1972, p. 93) puts it, authenticity in the "museum" setting is where experts

> test whether objects of art are what they appear to be or are claimed to be, and therefore worth the price that is asked for them – or, if this has already been paid, worth the admiration they are being given.

The consequence was that "the idea of being able to guarantee authenticity became vital when evaluating assets," and much effort was put into making sure "Artworks, rare books and other examples of material culture" were tested in a way so that they "could be affirmed as genuine" (du Cros and McKercher 2020, p. 99). Thus, "it is mainly [this] museum-linked usage which has been extended to tourism" (Wang 1999, pp. 350–351), such as if the intangible and tangible assets on display are 'authentic' or not. The implications of this perspective are that any reproduction or re-enactment is inherently inauthentic, and it completely ignores the perspectives of tourists and those in the tourism industry who are not museum professionals or historians.

Returning to Bruner, he says that

> the museum professionals acknowledge that New Salem is a reproduction, not an original; but they want that the reproduction to be authentic in the sense of giving the appearance of being like the 1830s . . . to produce a historic site believable to the public, to achieve mimetic credibility.
>
> (Bruner 1994, p. 399)

The New Salem site also includes one sense of authenticity as "duly authorized, certified, or legally valid," a definition which his site of New Salem meets due to its approval by the Illinois state government and being the only official one (ibid). This sense "is always present in the background, at least for museum professionals, insiders, locals, and scholars," yet tourists themselves are usually unaware of this (ibid). Bruner also defines a type of authenticity as 'genuineness' (Bruner 1994, p. 399), which would mean someone from, say, Venice, would look at the Venetian Macau and say 'this looks like Venice', or someone from Qing Dynasty-era China would say a reconstruction of the Summer Palace 'looks like' the original.

Further, those such as MacCannell (1973) argue that tourists do indeed search for authenticity and authentic experiences but are thwarted because their search is instead met with the 'staged authenticity' of the tourist sites. Indeed, other research has found as much, "For cultural tourists, object-related authenticity has a significant direct positive effect on tourist loyalty, but existentialist authenticity has no significant direct positive effect on tourist loyalty" (Chen and Zhou 2018, p. 70). Wang argues that "objective authenticity affects tourists' satisfaction," but then adds a caveat that is it "authenticity perception," which affects the satisfaction of tourists, not objective authenticity itself (Wang 2021, p. 133).

This mimics the positivist/Realist debates described earlier, where the focus is on removing whatever it is that is blocking us from experiencing reality. For science, it is developing better instruments and technology to more accurately collect data about what is really out there, be it information about chemicals and materials or statistical data about society and economics. For journalism, it was about removing bias and politics from news organizations and establishing codes of conduct and professional standards, in the end to better act as a mirror of Reality (Hearns-Branaman 2016). For tourism, it is about, as mentioned, the authentic nature of the artefacts in museums, and later on, for example, ensuring that 'locals' or 'natives' are the ones in charge of creating the tangible cultures such as clothing and food, or intangible cultures such as performances like dancing and singing.

This has led to a kind of dead end for Realist approaches for many fields and the move to social constructionist or Antirealist epistemological frameworks, as will be discussed in the next section. Cohen (1988) argues that the conclusion of many tourism researchers, that touristic commoditization leads to inescapable inauthenticity is "far-fetched and hard to accept" as it would also need us to have a view of "moderns society as completely absurd and dominated by sinister powers, so that its members are surreptitiously misled to believe that they have genuinely authentic experiences" (Cohen 1988, p. 373). For tourism, as Wang argues "To view authenticity as the original or the attribute of the original is too simple to capture its complexity" (Wang 1999, p. 353). Objects may be objectively Real but what about experiences? The move from cultural assets to products inevitably leads to staged authenticity as assets cannot be consumed and products, by their very nature, are staged. It is more fruitful to study how authenticity is constructed or co-constructed by the social interaction of tourists on one side and locals, natives, and various tourism workers on the other.

Antirealism

> Tourists want authentic experience, but do not necessarily want to experience reality. . . . Authenticity is a social construct that is determined in part by the individual's own knowledge and frame of reference.
>
> (du Cros and McKercher 2015, p. 115).

The dominant epistemological theory in contemporary tourism studies, as well as other cultural and communication-related fields, is here defined as

Antirealism. Otherwise, it has been defined as social constructivism by the likes of Schutz (1967) who argues that reality emerges through a competition between different discourses. Foucault relates this to discourse as well, arguing that "effects of truth are produced within discourses which in themselves are neither true nor false" (1980, p. 188). Philosophically, this can be expressed as: "whether or not there is an observer-independent reality can never be definitively confirmed" because "reality arises through the structure of a society and its specific culture" (Poerksen 2008, p. 296). The purpose is to decentre reality because "no one philosophical system or vantage point can grasp the plurality of discourses, institutions, or modes of power in modern society" (Mirchandani 2005, p. 91).

Wang (1999) gives a very apt description of different ways this is expressed. "Constructivists hold a pluralistic and relativist epistemology" and claim "that the validity of knowledge is not to be found in the relationship of correspondence to an independently existing world" (Wang 1999, p. 354). Wang, citing those such as Bruner (Bruner 1994) and Hobsbawm and Ranger (1983), gives several other criteria, that

- "there is no absolute and static original or origin on which the absolute authenticity of originals relies";
- "the construction of traditions or origins involves power and hence a social process";
- "authenticity or inauthenticity is a result of how one sees things and of his/her perspectives and interpretations";
- "authenticity is a label attached to the visited cultures in terms of stereotyped images and expectations held by the members of tourist-sending society"; and
- "even though something can initially be 'inauthentic' or 'artificial', it may subsequently become 'emergent authenticity' with the passage of time."

(Wang 1999, p. 355)

This is certainly the established framework from which to view the social construction of authenticity in tourism, yet points 2 to 5 also point to the limitations of such a framework. Emotions, perspectives, interpretations, and stereotyped images have no relationship to an underlying reality and thus have no relationship to epistemology. They are better described as Antirealist as they bracket out discussions of underlying reality and instead focus on signs and images of reality created by human action, manipulation of signifying systems which function to give signs of reality. Authenticity is not socially constructed; signs of authenticity are socially constructed. Wang (1999, 356, emphasis in original) as much as points that out: "tourists are indeed in search of authenticity; however, what they quest for is not objective authenticity (i.e., authenticity as originals) but *symbolic* authenticity which is the result of social construction." Yet as with most social constructivist arguments, the implications of this are not explored in greater detail.

Cohen (1988) gives a detailed elaboration and conceptualization of the social construction of authenticity in tourism. He argues " 'authenticity' is a socially constructed concept and its social (as against philosophical) connotation is, therefore, not given, but 'negotiable'" (Cohen 1988, p. 374). Tourists can "conceive 'authenticity' in different degrees of strictness" in that "individuals who are less concerned with the authenticity of their touristic experiences, will be more prepared to accept as 'authentic' a cultural product or attraction which more concerned tourists, applying stricter criteria, will reject as 'contrived'" (Cohen 1988, p. 376). It is negotiable because it is subjective to individual tourists, so "authenticity-eager" ones "may tend to idealize the destination, and thus eagerly embrace as genuine the very prevarications with which they are served" (Cohen 1988, p. 377). Thus, it relies not on the objective qualities of the tourist space but on the interpretation of the space by tourists who may or may not have a great deal of knowledge about the culture in question to judge its authenticity and accuracy. Furthermore, the negotiability of authenticity allows for the "gradual emergence" of some kind of authenticity "in the eyes of visitors to the host culture" in that "a cultural product, or a trait thereof, which is at one point generally judged as contrived or inauthentic may, in the course of time, become generally recognized as authentic" (Cohen 1988, p. 379).

Cohen's example is "an apparently contrived, tourist-oriented festival" which "may in due time become accepted as an 'authentic' local custom" (Cohen 1988, p. 379). This is an important point about how we conceptualize authenticity, as Cohen puts scare quotes around 'authentic' because it is 'socially constructed' and not 'objectively authentic.' What is being described is Antireal, from our conceptualization, because the contrived festival turned local custom has its origins in commercialized tourism and the manipulation of signs, not in the lived reality of the locals.

A constructivist, or relativistic view, can be seen in Bruner (1994). For example, when talking about the clothing worn by the employees at a historical reconstruction site, he notes that in the 1930s they wore jeans, yet in the 1990s the increasing popularity of visitors wearing jeans forces the employees to change their clothing. Those "who play the parts of the original residents" need to be distinguished from the tourist who come to visit, as "proper 1830s dress in 1930 is not proper in 1990" (Bruner 1994, p. 402). The great irony is that "what was considered authentic in the sense of credible in one historical era has changed in the course of 60 years" (Bruner 1994, p. 402). In other words, authenticity is relative, dependent not on the actual referents of history but socially constructed notions that are constantly in flux. The New Salem site created new and more diverse types of 1830s-style clothing, after an internal debate about "the issue of credibility" with the visitors, not about "what genuinely existed in the 1830s" (Bruner 1994, p. 403). Tourists do not actually want to see the authentic styles of the past if it conflicts with their stereotyped images of the past if it does not give off enough signs of difference from the present.

Bruner also questions the gap between the quality of the replication of the tangible cultural heritage product on display and the intangible qualities that are not able to be replicated:

> Even if the log houses in the 1990s prairie village were an exact physical replica of the original 1830s, in every detail, the question could then be raised: How does one make authentic the sensory mode of experiencing and indeed the very meaning of the site?
>
> (Bruner 1994, p. 404)

The answer is, of course, that tourists either have to construct their own meaning of authenticity or that the tourists do not really care about authenticity, and they just want an excuse to get out of the house. A re-created historical site is the perfect alibi, as it is educational and a part of American history, and its objective authenticity is unimportant. As Burner (1994, pp. 410–411) puts it:

> Tourists construct a past that is meaningful to them and that relates to their lives and experiences, and this is the way that meanings are constructed at historical sites. . . . The particular pasts that tourists create/imagine at historic sites may never have existed. But [they] do provide visitors with the raw material (experiences) to construct a sense of identity, meaning, attachment, and stability.

Tourism literature is replete with this kind of analysis, Nuryanti arguing that "Meaning lies in the observer or participant (i.e. the tourist) rather than as some objective quality inherent in the object itself" (Nuryanti 1996, p. 253), Urry and Larson that "there is no simple 'authentic' reconstruction of history but that all involve accommodation and reinterpretation" (Urry and Larson 2011, p. 146), Chhabra *et al.* (2003) that "satisfaction with a heritage event depends not on its authenticity in the literal sense of whether or not it is an accurate re-creation of some past condition, but rather on its perceived authenticity" (Chhabra *et al.* 2003, p. 705), "Authenticity is culturally defined, not a concept that can be scientifically and objectively measured and universally applied" (Li and Sofield 2009, p. 166).

The main takeaway from these Antirealist conceptions is that there is no Real authenticity for tourism, that it all perceptions and feelings of authenticity are co-created by tourists and others, such as locals and tourism workers. This then becomes a discussion of representation and is no longer an epistemological discussion as it has no connection to discussions about the relationship of tourism to Reality. As Wang says, "Constructivists are reluctant to dig a tomb for 'authenticity' and they try to rescue the term by revising its meanings; postmodernists have buried it" (Wang 1999, p. 358).

From Antirealism to Hyperrealism

It is this dismissive attitude towards postmodern approaches that has stymied the development of more innovative approaches to authenticity in tourism. Part of this lies in the interpretation of postmodern scholars by tourism scholars such as Wang and Bruner. Wang's interpretation of the 'postmodernist' approach to tourism, especially in regard to Baudrillard, is that the implication of the approach is a "justification of the contrived, the copy, and imitation" (Wang 1999, p. 357). Wang's example is of Cohen (1995), who posits a split between 'modern' tourists who still search for authenticity and 'postmodern' ones who enjoy the simulacra and praise 'staged authenticity' as a way to protect the authentic culture of the locals/natives. However, as we have argued, staged authenticity is the baseline, the consequence of converting cultural assets into products.

Thus, we are all, by default, 'postmodern tourists' simply due to the nature of mass tourism. One does not need to "justify the inauthenticity in tourist space" (Wang 1999, p. 358) when the authentic and inauthentic have imploded. Signs of authenticity are all that there is and they neither need to be justified nor condemned.

Wang's (1999) solution is 'existential authenticity,' which is detached from "the issue of whether toured objects are real" or not and is part of a "search of tourist experience which is existentially authentic, tourists are preoccupied with an existential state of Being activated by certain tourist activities" (Wang 1999, p. 359). Wang's immediate example is dance, where the authenticity or lack thereof is unimportant to the tourists' enjoyment of the activity or performance, or more generally speaking, their usage of tourism to cross boundaries to 'find' themselves. This is, however, still not an epistemological theory.

Bruner (1994) also entirely dismisses postmodernists like Baudrillard and Eco. Yet, if we re-examine Bruner we can find he actually has a misreading of Baudrillard and, ironically, many of these findings act to support Baudrillard's Hyperrealist theory.

Bruner gives a slight misreading of Eco and Baudrillard, saying that they imply "copies are based on originals" (Bruner 1994, p. 409). For Baudrillard at least, copies are based on copies, not originals. The issue is not that the replica of Venice in Las Vegas is an inauthentic copy and that is bad, and the replica of the Las Vegas Venetian in Macau is doubly inauthentic; the issue is that the Venetian Macau is a copy of the Las Vegas Venetian, which is a copy of Italian Venice which is a copy of people's stereotypes of Venice, and at all levels influenced more by media than by people's actual travels to Venice.

He also confuses their description, sometimes given ironically, about the quality of the reproductions. "Postmodern writers say that in hyperreality the reproduction is better than the original" (Bruner 1994, p. 397). Bruner argued that authors like Baudrillard and Eco, while stating that there is 'no original' in postmodern society, their work has an "implicit original," Europe (Bruner

1994, p. 398), in that Baudrillard and Eco's writings (i.e. Baudrillard 1989; Eco 1986) focused on a postmodern analysis of the USA with an implicit contrast and comparison to Europe. This approach, however, takes these works in isolation from the authors' larger body of work and poststructuralist theory.

Indeed, as we discussed earlier, the museum professionals in Bruner's study themselves had mixed feeling about the authenticity of their site, with those leaning towards 'genuineness' relying on "historical scholarship," actual personal letters and government documents from the period "to achieve authenticity" (Bruner 1994, pp. 399–400). At the same time, these methods seem very inauthentic as citizens of the 1830s New Salem did not do such things to learn about their lives; they actually lived their lives and left behind records of certain things; they did not make dresses and soap to demonstrate craft skills or create items to sell to tourists; they made them to wear and to clean things and therefore if their methods are 'authentic or not matters very little as the actual historical context of the actions has disappeared.

> New Salem is thus presented as a village of autonomous homes and isolate individuals, without any sense of group or community activity. . . . The result is that 1830s life is devoid of group character and is presented much more like 1990s suburban life in America, where neighbors live in their individual homes and are socially isolated from one another.
>
> (Bruner 1994, p. 404)

Yet, would the solution be to increase interactivity of the actors? That would simply involve them giving signs of being communal and social and would still be acting. Or to give actual stakes for their lives, such as starvation from a bad harvest or sick animals? This is completely unsustainable and is something that the visitors would not expect nor want. Therefore, this is a necessary, unavoidable inauthenticity.

Bruner's main contention against 'postmodernism' is that hyperrealism is not new,

> the simulacrum becomes the true, the copy becomes the original or even better than the original . . . all we have is pure simulacra, for origins are lost, or are not recoverable, or never existed, or there was no original reality.
>
> (Bruner 1994, p. 407)

Bruner says this is not a postmodern idea, as Baudrillard argues, "one specific to our electronic era," but "this is the human condition, for all cultures continually invent and reinvent themselves" (Bruner 1994, p. 407). He goes on to argue the position of Baudrillard and Eco is much closer to his 'constructivist' position, as well as a range of other epistemological theories such as the American pragmatism of Dewey and Mead, to the dialectics of Bakhtin, and poststructuralism like Barthes. This contention, however, unnecessarily collapses the very different views these schools of thought have about truth and authenticity, with Bruner saying the basic position of ALL of these philosophies is that "the meaning of the text is not inherent in the text but emerges from how people read or experience the text" and that socialization is at best an imperfect mechanism for cultural transmission" because "each new performance or expression of cultural heritage is a copy in that it always looks back to a prior performance" while maintaining originality in that such performances adapt to "new circumstances and conditions" (Bruner 1994, p. 407).

For our case of the Macau Venice and Las Vegas Venice, this would be to say it is unfair to call them inauthentic, they are original 'new performances' copying the previous performance of Italian Venice, which is itself not original and consists of new performances of the previous version of Venice. His relativistic, constructivist position thus immunizes sites like Macau Venice and Las Vegas Venice from any criticism.

In order to better illustrate how the implications of Hyperrealist theory can be applied to tourism, in the next section we will go back through the roots via Benjamin, McLuhan, Boorstin, and Baudrillard.

Hyperrealism

> America is neither dream nor reality. It is hyperreality. It is a hyperreality because it is a utopia which has behaved from the very beginning as though it were already achieved. Everything here is real and pragmatic, and yet it is all the stuff of dreams too.
>
> (Baudrillard 1989, pp. 28–29)

As mentioned earlier, very few studies of tourism embrace postmodernism fully, and even fewer use Baudrillard, the exceptions being Hom (2010, 2015) and Sakwit (2021). For example, Sakwit argues that a "simulation attempts to devour the real" because "signs of the real . . . become the real itself," and as a consequence "the difference between the real and unreal becomes blurred, or even irrelevant" (Sakwit 2021, p. 62). It is this 'irrelevance' that is key, we can no longer differentiate the 'real' and the 'unreal,' nor should we try. Yet the purpose should not be simply to examine the typical poststructuralist obsession of representation, such as how the commodification of assets to products in tourist sites necessitates the representation of only certain aspects of the 'original' asset and accept that the process is imperfect but necessary.

The purpose should be to show how this commodification process displaces the entire signification process to the point that all we can do is to consume signs and all we want to do is to consume signs. Yes, it is impossible to consume the 'raw asset,' despite the marking and rationale for these attractions being consumption of the 'raw' asset; and yes, tourists might claim to want authenticity and an authentic experience, but this is simply their alibi for travel as the authenticity they seek is of commodified tourist products, not the raw assets.

Tourists in Mt Yunji or Huitong Village do not really want to live in the original traditional villages, but they want to consume signs of that kind of life and history made famous by the media. Tourists in Splendid China and Window to the World just want to wonder in awe at the miniaturized replicas of places made famous via the media, and they obviously know they're not travelling around the world. Tourists in Hallstatt Huizhou and Macau Venice just want to consume signs of famous European tourist spots because they're supposed to consume these signs made famous by the media. The sites act to produce signs for tourists to consume. The 'authenticity' of the signs is immaterial and irrelevant, the signs of authenticity are an alibi, an excuse for the tourist site to exist and for the tourists to visit there.

We will now elaborate upon this by first examining Benjamin's theory concerning mechanical reproduction. Second, McLuhan's Medium is the Message theory will be applied to tourism, and finally, Boorstin's pseudo-event theory will be explored.

Mechanical Reproduction

Benjamin's basic thesis is that our advancing technical ability to create increasingly accurate reproductions of art, and by extension other cultural products, has the consequence of disempowering them. "Even the most perfect reproduction of a work of art is lacking in one element: its presence in time and space, its unique existence at the place where it happens to be" (Benjamin 1936, §2). This nexus of a unique presence in time and space is termed an aura. The consequence of increased reproducible art means that "the reproduced object" has been removed "from the domain of tradition," and thus, its power is reduced (Benjamin 1936, §2). This is viewed by him as potentially positive, as at the time he was writing the essay the rise of fascism in Europe was accompanied by increased reproducible art, such as propaganda posters and movies. Others (see Taylor and Harris 2008) have viewed it as more negative, as the loss of the deep meaning of cultural objects would have a devastating fact on culture and creativity.

Benjamin's theory alone can be readily applied to the aforementioned discussion on cultural assets and products, as the move from cultural assets to products is parallel to his concerns about reproductive technology. He mentions commodification as well: "As individual instances of artistic production become emancipated from the context of religious ritual, opportunities for displaying the products increase" (Benjamin 1936, §V). Whereas before most art could be seen in a specific place and time, like a religious icon only displayed during a special event or a painting in a lord's manor, reproductive technology removes those constraints. The same happens with tourism: works of art of all types, historical artefacts, and the like are moved into museums and art galleries for the masses to consume, and well-stocked museums and galleries become one of the largest magnets for tourists. Now one does not have to go to hike up into the hills in the searing afternoon sun to see a famous statue hidden in some ruins, one can silently contemplate it in a climate-controlled white-walled museum as the statue has been liberated. And you can view a whole series of statues, pottery, and other artworks from around the world in quick succession all in the space of an afternoon. Tourism removes the power from these cultural assets by changing their unique place in time and space by separating the tangible asset from its specific role in intangible cultural practices.

Baudrillard gives a structuralist-inspired reading of Benjamin (1936) by defining three orders of simulacra, which he ties to "the successive mutations of the law of value since the Renaissance" (Baudrillard 1976, p. 50). Pre-Renaissance, the 'obligatory sign' ruled because societies were based on ceremony and rank, thus "signs are not arbitrary" and their "circulation is restricted" as they are "protected by a prohibition that ensures their total clarity and confers an unequivocal status on each" (ibid.). Post-Renaissance signs became 'emancipated signs,' correlated to the emancipation of class and the rise of democratic ideals (ibid. 50–51). Signs are now 'arbitrary', and "the signifier starts to refer to a disenchanted universe of the signified, the common denominator of the real world, towards which no-one any longer has the least obligation" (ibid: 50). Thus, in the period from the Renaissance to the Industrial Revolution we have "overt competition at the level of signs of distinction" in the form of 'fashion,' something that cannot exist pre-Renaissance due to the tight control on signification. Instead of the production of signs being based on reciprocal social obligations, tradition, and class, they are now proliferate based on "demand" (ibid. 51).

The next order of simulacra, corresponding to Benjamin's 'Age of Mechanical Reproduction' (Benjamin 1936), arises during the Industrial Revolution, featuring "signs with no caste tradition, that will never have known restriction on their status, and which will never have to be counterfeits, since from the outset they will be products on a gigantic scale" (Baudrillard 1976, p. 55). Mass production of objects solves the problems caused by their counterfeiting. Instead of the relationship between objects being based on the original vs the counterfeit (i.e. real grapes vs stucco grapes), the relationship becomes that of "equivalence and indifference" as objects become "indistinct simulacra of one another" (ibid.). Benjamin's analysis thus "shows that reproduction absorbs the process of production, changes its goals, and alters the status of the product and the producer" (ibid.). In this order of simulacra, objects are

> conceived according to their very reproducibility, their diffraction from a generative core called a 'model'. . . . There is no more counterfeiting of an original . . . and no more pure series. . .; there are models from which all forms proceed according to modulated differences.
>
> (ibid. 56)

Thus, the result of "this process of reproducibility" is that the Real becomes "not only that which can be reproduced, but that which is always already reproduced: the hyperreal" (ibid. 73).

Baudrillard (1976, p. 55) argues that signs now work as part of a series: "The relation between [objects] is no longer one of an original and its counterfeit, analogy or reflection, but is instead one of equivalence and indifference" where "objects become indistinct simulacra of one another." This problematizes our notions of 'production' as well. He argues that production is not "the process at the origin of all others" but instead is "serial production," "a process which reabsorbs every original being and introduces a series of identical beings" and thus is produced through "models" (ibid: 55–56). Drawing from Benjamin's argument that "[t]he reproduced work of art is, to an ever-increasing extent, the reproduction of a work of art designed for reproducibility" (1936, §IV), Baudrillard posits that objects are "conceived through their very reproducibility" and "their diffraction from a generative core called a 'model'" (Baudrillard 1976, p. 65).

In the end, such reproduced culture is "anti-auratic" because our signs "do not proclaim their uniqueness but are mechanically, electronically and digitally reproduced and distributed" (Urry and Larson 2011, p. 98). Culture represented in tourism suffers from the same fate; it is reproduced at an exceptional rate, separated from realms of tradition and disempowered by its nature as a commodity.

Medium Is the Message

The second important aspect is the impact of technology on our relationships with other people. As McLuhan says, the medium is the message "because it is the medium that shapes and controls the scale and form of human association and action" (McLuhan 1964, p. 9). The medium, in our case, is mass tourism and commodified tourism products. For tourism, the social relations we get with mass commodified tourism are different in 'scale and form' than that of travel. The scale has increased almost globally as people in affluent countries and affluent people worldwide can access international networks of hotels and transportation (flights, trains, busses, taxis, hiking trails, etc.) to go to nearly any location they like. The tourist–local/native relationship has changed to one of monetary exchange, peppered with the customary welcoming and friendly attitude via emotional labour.

Channelling McLuhan, Baudrillard argues that "communication is no longer achieved through a symbolic medium, but a technical one: this is what makes it communication" (Baudrillard 1970b, p. 68). This is not only for communication in the sense of interpersonal communication via social media, but for how cultural meaning and difference is communicated. Baudrillard continues, arguing that "all the contents of meaning are absorbed in the dominant form of the medium," and because the "medium alone makes the event" this means that there is an "implosion of the medium and the real in a sort of nebulous hyperreality where even the definition and the distinct action of the medium are no longer distinguishable" (Baudrillard 1978b, pp. 100–101). The message and the medium of tourism have imploded; tourism is about tourism itself, the scale reaching around the globe, and our relationships with each other based on capital, not community.

Pseudo-Events

Boorstin argues that, due to the growth of mass media in the nineteenth century, an increasingly large audience necessitated an increase in the amount of information being transmitted. This caused, in his example, journalists to have to find more events to turn into stories. If the events cannot be found, then their goal was to contrive the production of events to be turned into stories. This could be in collaboration with politicians, such as conducting an interview, with public relations experts, such as covering a press conference, or with promotional media experts by covering their events where are created to be covered by the media, such as product launches or public demonstrations. Boorstin labels these as 'pseudo-events,' events that exist only to create content for journalists to convert into stories, and defined them by four characteristics. First, it is an event that "is not spontaneous" in that it has been "planned, planted or incited" by an interested party, in opposition to an accident or natural disaster (Boorstin 1961, p. 11). Furthermore, pseudo-events are "planted primarily (not always exclusively) for the immediate purpose of being reported or reproduced" and has the "convenience" of the news media and its widespread reportage as one of its main concerns (Boorstin 1961, p. 11). Third, and perhaps most importantly, "[i]ts relation to the underlying reality of the situation is ambiguous" and that the interest in it "arises largely from this very ambiguity" (Boorstin 1961, p. 11). The interest now extends from a discussion of the event's nature, "in whether it really happened and in what might have been the motives" (Boorstin 1961, p. 11).

Finally, in the end it tends to be nothing more than a "self-fulfilling prophecy"; the celebration of the "distinguished hotel" is what makes the hotel "distinguished" (Boorstin 1961, p. 12) or the interview with the 'influential' personality further enshrines their influence. As Baudrillard argues, following Boorstin, "in earlier times an event was something that happened – now it is something designed to happen . . . as a reflection of pre-existing media-defined forms" (Baudrillard 1993, p. 41).

This causes uncertainty about the nature of events and experiences in our lives because these pseudo-events "flood our consciousness" yet are "neither true nor false in the old familiar senses" (Boorstin 1961, p. 36). Since events, performances, and the like are created with the media and the audience in mind this has made them "more vivid, more impressive, and more persuasive than reality itself" (Boorstin 1961, p. 36). The tourist gaze is created due to separation of the tourists' everyday life and something special in the places tourists visit. (Urry and Larson 2011, p. 15). This might be, for example, a "unique object" that is "absolutely distinct," which "everyone knows about," and which is "famous for being famous."

Tourist sites often can become famous for being famous. While the design of the Eiffel Tower itself is generally accepted as being unique and aesthetically pleasing, a massive monument to modernism and communication placed at the end of the Champ de Mars, this cannot be the only reason for its fame. Its construction caused a lot of controversy at the time due to its grandiosity and modern design, and the subsequent public discussion in cafes and newspapers put it on the minds of the public not only in Paris and in France but around the world. This extra attention, not simply the nature of the tower itself, is what made it rise to prominence and become a symbol of Paris and a first-class tourist attraction, although the controversy behind it is no longer the reason for its popularity. It is famous for being famous.

Wang (1999) criticizes Boorstin's (1961) take on tourism, claiming Boorstin sees tourists as "gullible" (Wang 1999, p. 352) for buying into the pseudo-events which make up commodified tourism, and argues that "Boorstin's concept of 'pseudo-events' implies a concept of objective authenticity" (Wang 1999, p. 353) and that he "scorns mass tourism and mass tourists" (ibid). However, we argue that Boorstin is not simply nostalgic for an authentic experience that did exist and was accessible and tourists are now being fooled. Boorstin is saying that mass tourism is an entirely different experience than 'travel,' tourists enjoy the pseudo-events that mass tourism offers, and there is no way to get back to an 'original.' Motivation to pursue authenticity does not assume that authenticity exists.

Uncertainty

Baudrillard brings together Benjamin's concerns about the effects of reproductive technology, McLuhan's observations on the implosion of the medium and the message, and Boorstin's pseudo-event concept to form the basis of his Hyperrealism theory. Sakwit interprets Baudrillard as conceiving authenticity as "the exchange of signification" which is "embedded in a combination of references" (Sakwit 2021, p. 57), quoting Baudrillard talking about the signifying properties of antique objects in that they lack "any practical application" and are "not functional," but instead have "a very specific function within the system, which is merely to signify" (Baudrillard 1996, p. 77).

The core of this is the notion of uncertainty: "An immense uncertainty is all that remains from the sophistication of networks of communication and information – the undecidability of knowing whether there is real knowledge or not, whether there is any real form of exchange or not" (Baudrillard 1992, pp. 22–23). The catch is that efforts are still made to distinguish lies from truth, the authentic from the inauthentic. Baudrillard argues that is part of the problem, "we hope to reduce this uncertainty with more information, with more communication, thereby reinforcing the uncertainty of the whole system" (Baudrillard 1992, pp. 22–23).

It is not to say that some tourist assets are inauthentic or authentic, for the difference between them is often impossible to distinguish, thus creating uncertainty. Authenticity is simulated in the sense that to "simulate is to feign to have what one hasn't" (Baudrillard 1978, p. 5).

The self-referential, pseudo-event nature of tourist assets means that they should be treated as "mythic operators" and not simply as "lairs" (Baudrillard 1975, p. 72) in the sense that fake items and practices are being presented as authentic. This is an important distinction in Hyperreality compared with Anti-realism, because if the representations "were merely liars, it would be easy to unmask them" by showing the inauthenticity, therefore we rely on "the invention of persuasive displays that are neither true nor false" (Baudrillard 1975, p. 72).

For tourism, this means that cultural assets that have been transformed into products should be viewed as being beyond inauthentic and authentic. If they are really inauthentic then it would be easy to discern; the colours on the clothing are not traditional, the steps in the dance do not follow the rules, the design of the building uses the wrong pattern or materials, the explanation of the folk tale has been misinterpreted. This certainly does happen in tourism, yet it is quite rare and easily exposed.

Instead, these cultural products give signs that they are authentic: the colour is right, the dance moves are spot on, the building's brickwork is intricate, and the folk tale illustrates the morals of the community perfectly. Yet because these cultural assets have been commodified for tourism they are driven from their original contexts and meanings. The clothing design is proper, but it is used as a costume in a restaurant to give signs of the culture and is not part of the original ceremonies it was intended for. The dancers are experts, but they are performing it for an audience as part of their job, not for joy as part of a community festival. The building's uniquely designed outside is the only thing that is left, and it only remains to give signs of the architectural style, the inside has been transformed into a business to serve tourists. The folktale used to be told to children as part of their socialization process, now it is translated into English and other languages and made as part of an exhibit about that area's oral traditions.

This is what we mean by pseudo-authenticity: authenticity that is beyond true and false and lives only to give signs of authenticity.

Pseudo-Authenticity

In this section, we will unpack the implications of the aforementioned discussion by elaborating on three analytic categories we will use in the remaining chapters to evaluate the influence of pseudo-authenticity on tourism. First, we will look at the influence of media on our stereotypes and images of places that we want to tour, in other words what we anticipate experiencing, how this influences our decoding of the signs we consume, and how we re-encode this through our tourism photography.

Media Influence

The perceived authenticity of the signs that tourists consume is influenced heavily by mediated signs of the consumed site the tourist consumed before travelling. These mediated signs of the site may be through tourist advertising, word-of-mouth of other tourists or locals, education (history, culture), or more likely movies and TV shows of the site, and more general perceptions of the region, culture, country, etc., the tourist travels to, based more on stereotypes and reputation, signs manipulated by the media. Many tourist sites are famous for being famous, as we discussed earlier with the Eiffel Tower.

As Culler (1981, p. 4) argues, the semiotic process of tourism "has a curious effect: the proliferation of markers or reproductions confers an authenticity upon what may at first seem egregiously inauthentic," and the impact of media cannot be underestimated, for example, with Los Angeles "the reproduction of its features in a variety of media, creates originals of which these reproductions are reproductions and a desire to see the signified of which these markers are signifiers" (Culler 1981, p. 132).

The "sacralization" of special tourist sites "often depends on texts and stories that circulate elsewhere or around the site" with the result that "our sense of having visited somewhere special is premised upon other signs and texts" (Crang 2004, p. 77). This is caused by the massive "mediatization" of tourism, certain tourist sites "proliferate across the globe" and consequently "everyday sites of activity get redesigned in 'tourist' mode, as with many themed environments" to follow the codes crafted by this mediatization (Urry and Larson 2011, p. 30).

This also relates to Bruner's (1994) concept of 'verisimilitude,' the criteria are that someone from right now would go to a reproduced historical site and say that this looks like what they "expected" the site to look like. It is possible to argue that these expectations come largely, if not almost entirely, from mass-mediated images like historical dramas on TV, documentaries, or even history textbooks.

We also draw from Urry and Larson's concept of the 'tourist gaze' here, in that it involves the "cognitive work of interpreting, evaluating, drawing comparisons and making mental connects between signs and their referents" as well as "capturing signs photographically" (Urry and Larson 2011, p. 17). Our media-influenced codes affect 1) what we anticipate to see in tourism, 2) how we decode the signs when we actually get there, and 3) how we encode the signs through our tourism photography.

Anticipation

Boorstin's chapter on tourism in his book *The Image* goes into a lot of detail about the changes in mass tourism. For him the modern tourist "looks for caricature" and as a consequence "travel agents at home and national tourist bureaus abroad are quick to oblige" (Boorstin 1961, p. 106). Tourists are led by their "own provincial expectations" for what to expect from their travels and "seldom likes the authentic (to him often unintelligible) product of the foreign culture" (Boorstin 1961, p. 106). Pocock argues, similarly, that "the power of secondary sources in general forge expectations and bolster the urge to travel" (Pocock 1992, p. 243). Pocock (1992) found that tourists visiting a UK town whose image was heavily influenced by a famous novel judged the authenticity of the site in comparison with their expectations based on the book. Following Campbell (1987), Urry and Larson (2011, pp. 50–51) point out that modern consumption often involves the consumer experiencing " 'in reality' the pleasurable dramas they have already experienced in their imagination." Tourists are looking for something special that distinguishes the visited place from their normal lives and do so by "reading the landscape for signifiers of certain preestablished notions or signs derived from discourses of travel and tourism" (Urry and Larson 2011, p. 15) following Culler 1981).

Chhabra, Healy, and Sills conceptualize this as "day dreaming and anticipation of new or different experiences"; however, it is "not autonomous" because it involves "working over advertising and other media-generated sets of signs" (Chhabra *et al.* 2003, p. 712). Their study finds the very same, that for a cultural heritage festival, the "perceived level of authenticity is controlled partly by media and partly by the people [tourists] themselves" (Chhabra *et al.* 2003, p. 715). Authenticity is "is a label attached to the visited cultures" by tourists not in the terms of the locals themselves but "in terms of stereotyped images and expectations held by the members of tourist-sending society" (Wang 1999, p. 355).

The "imaginative geographies" of tourism can feel "so real" for tourists because they are "built upon convictions of 'actualities'" such as "views, national types and buildings" (Urry and Larson 2011, p. 176). This creates a "visual grammar" made of "a seductive mix of reverie, reality and fiction" in which our preconceptions of tourist sites are both naturalized and fictionalized (Urry and Larson 2011, p. 176). Tourist sites like those with "themed environments" depend on simulating signs that are "predictable and well-known" to tourists, relying on "a limited array of features" which are then "exaggerated" but in the end "finally come to dominate over other senses" (Urry and Larson 2011, p. 125).

du Cros and McKercher are more moderate, arguing instead that the tourist "may be travelling to have their stereotypical or romantic images of a destination reinforced" while others may want it "challenged" (du Cros and McKercher 2015, p. 115). Yet they still admit that most of the previous knowledge of tourists "would have likely come from the mass media, documentary and lifestyle television shows, and the cinema," and this kind of "information often presents a distorted vision" (du Cros and McKercher 2015, p. 115).

Decoding

When tourists arrive at their destinations their sense of authenticity of the site is thus based on their decoding of the signs of the site based on their previous knowledge and stereotypes. Tourists also bring "their mindsets, routines and social relations" with them on their travels, "thereby the imaginative geographies of tourism are as much about 'home' as faraway places" (Haldrup and Larsen 2010, p. 27). Boorstin (1961, p. 116) gives an example of this from how travel literature has changed:

> Formerly these books brought us information about the conduct of life in foreign courts, about burial rites and marriage customs, about the strange ways of beggars, craftsmen, tavern hosts, and shopkeepers. . . . travel books have increasingly become a record not of new information but of personal 'reactions.' From 'Life in Italy,' they become 'The American in Italy.' People go to see what they already know is there. The only thing to record, the only possible source of surprise, is their own reaction. The foreign country . . . is the confirmation of a pseudo-event.

He goes on to argue that our interest in travelling is influenced by "whether our impression" of the site "resembles the images found in the newspapers, in moves, and on television" (Boorstin 1961, p. 116). Our experiences are thus shallow and dependent more on our own stereotypes of the place instead of the place itself. "We go not to test the image by the reality, but to test reality by the image" (Boorstin 1961, p. 116). We go "to see what [we] already know is there," thus the "only thing to record, the only possible source of surprise, is [our] own reaction" (Boorstin 1961, p. 116).

This influences the tourism providers as well. Sawkit gives the example of the food served in floating markets in Bangkok and Pattaya, Thailand. The food offered is "not local specialty dishes" from Pattaya but more "generic Thai dishes" (like Tum Yong Gang and mango sticky rice) that would be more well-known to international tourists, and in addition, the taste is "altered to suit Chinese tourists' taste" as they are the dominant tourist group (Sakwit 2021, pp. 118–119). Eventually such generic dishes become universally expected to be served at restaurants in Thailand and Thai restaurants globally, new restaurants are expected to have these generic dishes on the menu, they become more generic, and thus 'authentic' Thai food. Irish Pubs in Ireland, and around the world, are expected to copy the American-style Irish Pubs to maintain their 'authenticity,' Italian pizza restaurants in Italy, and around

Europe and the world, are expected to copy the commercialized American Pizza Hut-style pizzas, etc.

Tourists may decode from specific experiences of recent popular culture that will inspire travel to certain places, like Florence after the film *Hannibal* (2001) or Bangkok after *The Hangover II* (2011), and the list can go on. Sakwit gives the example of the 2010 Chinese film *Go Lala Go!*, part of which was filmed in the Pattaya floating market. "Tourists decode the reality of the floating market in accordance with the code given in the messages" of the film (Sakwit 2021, pp. 121–122). The market itself has to embrace its presence in the movie by adopting many of the movie's codes, especially in regard to package tours aimed at Chinese tourists which benefit by including the market in their itinerary (Sakwit 2021, pp. 120–122).

Tourism Photography

> [Photography's] main effect is to convert the world into a department store or a museum-without-walls in which every subject is depreciated into an article of consumption, promoted into an item for aesthetic appreciation.
>
> (Sontag 1979, p. 110)

After arriving at the tourists' destination, we then proceed to document our trip photographically. Photography is intimately tied to the growth of tourism, Kodak's early marking campaigns and the development of cameras developed for tourists (see Urry and Larson 2011). Osborne notes "the ultimate inseparability" of photography "from tourism's general culture and economy and from the varieties of modern culture of which they are constitutive" (Osborne 2000, p. 70).

But our tourism photography is not something independent and reliant on the tourists' own photographic creativity. We have "obligations" with our photography: "People feel that they must not miss seeing particular scenes or 'Kodak moments' since otherwise the photo-opportunities will be missed and forgotten" (Urry and Larson 2011, p. 178). If we miss taking photo of the buildings and attractions that we are supposed to take photos of, then our posting on social media afterwards will seem incomplete. How can one travel to Paris without taking a photo of the Eiffel Tower, to Bangkok without taking a photo of the notoriously hard-to-photograph Reclining Buddha in Wat Pho, or the typical photo of holding up the Leaning Tower of Pisa in Italy?

Urry and Larson thus argue that we are seeking to take "a set of photographic images which have already been seen in brochures, TV programmes, blogs and social networking sites" (Urry and Larson 2011, p. 179). Our job involves "tracking down and capturing those images for oneself" and to demonstrate to our friends and family that we "really have been there" by capturing the images that everyone knows and has seen countless times (Urry and Larson 2011, p. 179).

Tourist sites happily oblige without efforts, including the placement of signs telling us that this is a good place to take a photo, or installing platforms to allow for a more scenic shot, conveniently providing a hashtag to help us promote their site on our social media. Thus, the internet and social media influence "tourism businesses and how tourists plan their journeys" in that they can "produce web content as well as consum[e] it" (Urry and Larson 2011, p. 59) via public reviews on booking and informational sites and apps, and in our public/private social media posts.

We thus encode the visited sites on the basis of the images that we are supposed to take photos of, often contrived views manipulated by the tourist site. The photos are taken to be shared, not for private consumption, to prove to others that we have seen the right things and thus validating out travels.

Authentic Fakery

> All tourist attractions share [a] factitious, pseudo-eventful quality. Formerly when the old-time traveler visited a country whatever he saw was apt to be what really went on there. . . . Folk song and folk dance were for the natives themselves. Now, however, tourist sees less of the country than of its tourist attractions. Today what he sees is seldom the living culture, but usually specimens collected and embalmed especially for him, or attractions specially staged for him: proved specimens of the artificial.
>
> (Boorstin 1961, p. 102)

The concept of authentic fakery refers to a phenomenon where a constructed or replicated experience is intentionally designed to imitate or simulate authenticity. It involves creating an experience that resembles an authentic cultural or historical site which gives signs of authentic tangible and intangible culture for tourists to consume. These destinations may not explicitly acknowledge their artificiality and offer visitors an opportunity to engage with cultural and historical elements in a controlled and accessible manner. It thus raises important questions about the commodification of culture, the loss of historical context, and the boundaries between authenticity and imitation in the tourism industry. This concept was developed via examining how communities stage different elements of their culture for outsiders and eventually applied to cultural tourism.

Here, we will show how the tourists' efforts to enter the 'back stage' of the locals' lives caused the locals to develop a fake backstage for the tourists' consumption.

Front-Stage vs Back-Stage

Staged authenticity (MacCannell 1973) is when a tourist site's images, aesthetics and cultural practices, for example, "are arranged to produce the impression that a back region has been entered even when this is not the case" (MacCannell 1973, p. 589). What tourists experience is not the actual 'backstage' representation of the historical sites, having the curtain pulled back to reveal what was once hidden. Instead, it is still a 'front-state' area dressed up to appear as if it is the back. Thus, tourists still can only experience what the tourist site operators want to reveal to them. Walby and Piché argue this kind of approach benefits from not being stuck in an authentic vs inauthentic dichotomy. Instead, it "suggests that what is distinctive about late twentieth century culture is the pervasiveness of performative, staged displays that are manipulated and used as a resource to facilitate safe, at-a-distance tourist experiences" (Walby and Piché 2015, p. 233).

This 'back region' is perceived to be more authentic than the 'front regions,' that is, "the meeting place of hosts and guests or customers and service person" (MacCannell 1973, p. 590), such as hotel lobbies, airports, and restaurants. Entering another generic, Western-looking building and sitting at another generic Western-looking table to eat generic Western-looking food will not excite any Western tourist. Instead, for example, the restaurant would be decorated to look like a traditional village with the waitstaff in traditional or ethnically themed clothing instead of formal Western waitstaff uniforms. The tourist thus feels as if they have pierced the veil and gone behind the scenes, when this authentic restaurant is constructed in order to keep the guests out of the real behind the scenes of the locals' everyday lives.

Van den Berghe (1980) gives a very thorough examination of this process by looking at tourism in 1970s Peru. He noted that a division grew between the native Peruvians, with the mestizo group becoming the 'middlemen,' due to their being more educated, middle-class, multilingual, and more Westernized (and thus not exotic enough for tourists), and the native Indian group becoming the tourees. Additionally, smaller towns in the countryside began "transforming their traditional town fiesta into a tourist pageant" to attract tourists, and thus income (van den Berghe 1980, p. 387). Thus, while tourists are "in search of the exotic" that is not achievable "under the onslaught of mass tourism" as the "exotic [quickly] becomes fake" (van den Berghe 1980, p. 380) in the move from cultural assets to products. He argues that the "tourist does not want to see touree" but instead "unspoiled natives" (ibid). Again, tourism products are necessarily 'spoiled' due to their commodification. Therefore in the end the touree/native is transformed into "a performer who modifies [their] behavior for gain according to what is attractive to the tourist" and "makes it [their] business of preserving a credible illusion of authenticity" (van den Berghe 1980, p. 380).

This can also be used for aesthetic purposes not directly involving people. Wang and Chen (2020) apply Cohen's (1979a, 1979b) staging authenticity categorization to analyse how combinations of sounds form different kinds of tourist experiences in Dong Village finding that language environment and symbolic sound environment are important yet often neglected in constructing an authentic experience for tourists (Wang and Chen 2020). The Terminal 21 international-themed shopping mall in Bangkok uses scents, piping in the smell of sakura on the Tokyo-themed floor and incense on the Istanbul-themed floor, to help give multisensory signs of having travelled around the world.

It can also be applied to the ethics of tourist facilities whose tangible assets have been radically modified into products to serve tourists. In researching Naxi Guesthouses in Lijiang in 2001, Wang found that despite the interviewees claiming that they were primarily seeking "an 'authentic' Naxi cultural experience" by "choosing a homestay in Lijiang" (Wang 2007, p. 792), the homestays had been modified so much to meet tourists needs that the owners themselves did not view their own guest houses as 'authentic.' Despite the 'staged' nature of the Naxi homestays, "its authenticity can still be perceived and even enjoyed by the guests" (ibid: 795) because the homestay's design on the surface level gives signs that you are peeking behind the scenes of the ethnic group's lives.

Several researchers even argue that heritage tourists in fact demand and require a certain level of staging of authenticity. Chhabra *et al.* (2003) argue that, while staging "involves displacement of cultural production from one place to another and modification to fit new conditions of time and place," it does not "preclude authenticity" because "what is staged is not superficial since it contains elements of the original tradition" (Chhabra *et al.* 2003, p. 704). Put in poststructuralist terms, this argument falls apart. The staged 'original traditional elements' are now simply signs of the 'original traditional elements.' The change in historical context, the inculcation of commercialism into tourism, and the specific demands of different kinds of tourists (middle-class, backpackers, families, etc.) necessitate a selective staging wherein elements are included and excluded.

Enjoying Fakery

> One invites the masses to participate, to simulate, and to play with the models – they go one better: they participate and manipulate so well that they efface all the meaning. Thus they become hypersimulated in response to cultural simulation and, in turn, become the agents of the execution of this culture.
>
> (Baudrillard 1994, p. 66).

MacCannell (1999) later argues that, in addition to 'staged authenticity,' tourist sites frequently feature what he terms 'authentic fakery.' Hom applies this to Las Vegas, arguing that tourists go there "to see the fake" and that "to experience the fake is to experience authentic Las Vegas" (Hom 2010, p. 381). This is in direct opposition to the discourse used by Las Vegas developers, yet it would seem odd if their PR teams promoted it as a place full of fakery. Tourists are, perhaps, in on the joke and really do not expect to find authentic Italy or France or Egypt in the deserts of Nevada, it is just an excuse to go there.

Even earlier, Cohen argued that "even the faintest vestige of, or resemblance to what experts would consider an 'authentic' trait of the product, may suffice for [tourists] to play the make-believe game of having an 'authentic' experience" (Cohen 1988, p. 379). Tourists would then "playfully consent to buy fake products or experiences as if they were genuine, merely because of their resemblance to the genuine thing gives these tourists an inkling of authenticity" (Cohen 1988, p. 379). This may not apply to all tourists, but certainly those "who are less concerned with the authenticity of their touristic experiences" have greater capacity to "to accept as 'authentic' a cultural product or attraction which more concerned tourists, applying stricter criteria, will reject as 'contrived'" (Cohen 1988, p. 376).

Tourists are not naïve and know of the artifice of their experience to some extent and do not want to jeopardize the time and money spent on their journey by being too serious about seemingly authentic objects and experiences presented to them by the locals for their consumption. Lash and Urry argue that the "post-tourist knows that he or she is a tourist, and tourism is simply a series of games with multiple texts and no single authentic experience," giving the example that we know the "the apparently local entertainment is as socially contrived as the ethnic bar" or that "the quaint traditional fishing village cannot survive without the income from tourism" (Lash and Urry 1994, p. 276). We acknowledge these kinds of situations and relationships, yet we are happy to oblige in order to protect the integrity of our travels.

As discussed earlier, tourists frame the consumption of signs through their "own provincial expectations" (Boorstin 1961, p. 106), to which Sakwit agrees, arguing that "authenticity may not be the most important goal for tourists, rather, they expect to see spurious objects and places" (Sakwit 2021, p. 35). A core element of this we have to remember is that tourism is a temporary and often unique experience for people. Tourists "may only visit an asset once in their lifetime, and consequently wish to get the most out of the experience" and therefore are quite "amenable to having the asset presented in a manner that facilitates easy consumption" (du Cros and McKercher 2015, p. 113). Once time and resources are devoted to travel, tourists would try to make the best of the situation even if the experience is not up to the standards that they imagined.

A good example of this comes from Sakwit, who found, through interviews with tourists, that they admitted even though they knew the tourist site was "constructed for tourists" they still argued it was "worth a visit" (Sakwit 2021, p. 83). Further, since the floating markets are a "'must-do' activity," tourists are, in a way, obligated to "follow the codes and norms of holidays" and not the specific cultural elements of the markets (Sakwit 2021, p. 84): that is just what you do when you go to Thailand, you go to a floating market, and the floating markets exist because that's what people do when they go to Thailand. This is not simply to say the floating markets are inauthentic due to their commodification, but that they have become pseudo-authentic through the manipulation of signs, that is, the presence of the floating markets in tourist marketing literature, tourism travel packages, word-of-mouth from previous visitors, and popular culture like movies, as discussed earlier.

Façadism

> As for the native, [they] can best escape tourist attention by dressing like a tourist. The process reaches its ultimate conclusion when the native sheds [their] traditional dress for everyday life and only selectively dons it when [they perform] for tourists. Traditional dress then becomes theatrical costume.
>
> (van den Berghe 1980, p. 380–381)

Contrasting with authentic fakery, the concept of façadism refers more to the external aesthetics of tangible cultural products. Façadism originally refers to the "retention of the original building's façade only" (du Cros and McKercher 2015, p. 33–34), indicating the valuation only of the extrinsic and aesthetic value of a tangible cultural heritage asset and the loss of the building's intangible heritage. They point out that cultural assets "can undergo near total transformation and still retain their authenticity as far as many tourists are concerned," their example being the "architectural compromise of preserving the façade of historic building designated for redevelopment" (du Cros and McKercher 2020, p. 145). In this case, the outside of a historical building will be preserved while the inside will be extensively renovated to make it modern, with appropriate health and safety infrastructure like fire suppression systems, Wi-Fi and internet, and similar facilities. The purpose of the inside might be changed as well, such as a religious or governmental building being changed into a hotel or restaurant.

Here, façadism will be extended to include the façades of not just buildings but the external experience of all tangible products, especially in relationship to their intangible aspects. If a cultural product only contains tangible elements and lacks any intangible culture, we can thus conceptualize it as a façade. As Urry and Larson (2011, p. 120) put it:

> Previous elements of high culture are mass-produced and no longer signify a stable style. This is an architecture of surfaces and appearances, of playfulness and pastiche. It is mannerist – as if all the historical styles and conventions of architecture are there to be endlessly drawn on, juxtaposed and drawn on yet again.

They define Hyperreal places as those which "are characterized by surface appearances" and in which any "sense of sight is condensed to the most immediate and visible aspects of the scene" (Urry and Larson 2011, p. 18).

UNESCO defines intangible cultural heritage to include "the practices, representations, expressions, knowledge, skills – as well as the instruments, objects, artifacts and cultural spaces associated therewith – that communities, groups and . . . individuals recognize as part of their cultural heritage," as well as providing people with "a sense of identity and continuity, thus promoting respect for cultural diversity and human creativity" (UNESCO 2003). Intangible culture requires people, that is, "the cooperation and participation of 'folk', 'tradition bearers', 'living treasures', 'shifus or masters/mistresses' and others is essential" – additionally "the setting is important, for intangible heritage is intrinsically linked to place" (du Cros and McKercher 2015, p. 84–86). Thus a façade, in our meaning, tends to lack in two specific aspects, 1) 'local' people and 2) relevant links to place.

People

Bruner's (1994) concept of 'historical verisimilitude' fits this distinction, in that it is defined as authenticity that comes from a reproduction that looks credible and convincing, in other words, a reproduction that efficiently gives signs of the original by creating a facade.

> Even if the log houses in the 1990s prairie village were an exact physical replica of the original 1830s, in every detail, the question could then be raised: How does one make authentic the sensory mode of experiencing and indeed the very meaning of the site?
>
> (Bruner 1994, p. 404)

That site lacks both people and place, and the tangible culture that is performed there, i.e. making butter and rope, while being done by people is not being done by locals or natives, instead by students or actors.

Du Cros and McKercher do note that "how to convert something that is essentially private and personal into something to be consumed by tourists" is the "greatest challenge" and "must lead to some compromises" (du Cros and McKercher 2020, p. 118). They give a possible solution as turning cultural "events into performances," which mitigates "adverse impacts" on the local community, but also has the effect of removing "much of the meaning and value" from the cultural practice (du Cros and McKercher: 118). They give the example of a replica of an American church in a cultural theme park in Dalian, China: "The physical structure of the church is an exact replica of the original, but the interior is devoid of any reference to Christianity" (du Cros and McKercher 2020, p. 119). Wedding packages are sold to locals who go to the church for a western-themed photo session, with the typical western wedding clothes and service, yet the experience is "completely lacking any of the associated intangible cultural significance and meaning associated with Christian weddings" (du Cros and McKercher 2020, p. 119).

In other words, the Chinese travellers go there to consume signs of a Western wedding and church experience, only the decontextualized façade of the tangible cultural traditions with the requisite intangible core. One might say this kind of practice is 'authentic' because of the co-construction of meaning between the tour operators, the tourists, and their families, and that they would view it as sufficiently authentic for their purposes. From a pseudo-authenticity perspective, however, the externally authentically aesthetic trappings of the situation are simply the alibi for the experience. The choice to have such an experience is informed by their consumption of signs of Western-style weddings from TV shows and movies, shares on social media, word-of-mouth from their acquaintances' past experience attending and planning weddings, and from brochures by wedding photographers and wedding planners which contain a variety of styles on offer.

Often, especially for historical sites, the location may be accurate, but there is no way to convey the experiences of the 'locals.' Walby and Piché (2015, p. 234) pointed out that some historical elements, in their instance abstract feelings and emotions like "human suffering and pain" that are part of carceral sites, are impossible to be authentic as they "cannot be physically reproduced" (Walby and Piché 2015, p. 234). All that's left of the site is the façade of a prison – barred doors, mess halls, and guard towers – and that is certainly all that the tourists want to consume of the whole enterprise. We will playfully consume signs of carceral experiences, such as being temporarily 'locked' in a cell for a photo op, but that's as far as it goes.

At other times, the place and people involved are modified to meet tourist demands to such an extent that they become autonomous and no longer connected to local culture outside of their tourist uses. Chhabra, Healy, and Sills argue that events like cultural heritage festivals are a blend of two cultural functions, as given by in that first "an attempt is made to copy the original; then the copy is modified to meet the needs of the modern community" (Chhabra *et al.* 2003, p. 704). Such events contain "sites, objects, images, and even people" which are "positioned as signifiers of past events, epochs, or ways of life," not "contemporaneous productions" (Taylor 2001, p. 33). Sakwit's (2021) study of floating markets in Thailand, mentioned earlier, being dislocated in place is also a good example as one market moved from their original location to a more accessible one while the other was constructed from scratch to make sure the setting was ideal for tourists. "Present-day floating markets are not an authentic representation of traditional Thai culture and local way of life, but rather a simulation, displaying an image of the country" (Sakwit 2021, p. 1). The merchant's boars cannot even be used as transportation, such as between the wholesale market and the public market as it was in the past.

Place

Place and its relationship to intangible culture has been raised as an area of concern because the deletion of intangible cultural heritage "from its physical and social setting," or if the setting never had any, could result in the "trivialization" of such culture "to the extent that it becomes little more than a hollow parody of itself" (du Cros and McKercher 2015, p. 95). Urry and Larson (2011) also noted the importance of place, that tourist services "cannot be provided anywhere; they have to be produced and consumed within specific places" (Urry and Larson 2011, p. 49). Indeed, what tourists often consume is "in effect, the place in which the service producers are located," yet "the quality of the specific service may be tarnished" if, for example, "the particular place does not convey appropriate cultural meaning and display memorable visual features" (Urry and Larson 2011, p. 49). This expectation by tourists causes the sites to emphasize on their outward appearance, for example, using typical materials associated with the culture, like bamboo or certain colours of brick, specific plants or flowers associated with the area, decorations like statues or paintings that represent local or regional culture, and other such aesthetic flourishes.

Returning to Sakwit's floating market, they argue that while the site "appears to be authentic, it is not in itself authentic" because "the floating market functions as a sign of nostalgia, namely local tradition and way of life" and, in the end, "what makes the place authentic" is "its association with the signification of time and the source of value" (Sakwit 2021, p. 91). The floating markets "are sold to tourists as commodities" and thus the consumed "cultural content" is not about use-value, or any "practical application" but instead depend on "sign-value" (Sakwit 2021, p. 109). The 'place' for the floating market is right, a series of rivers and canals with boats where people go shopping. Yet for the tourist versions we can only consume signs of the place and this behaviour as the canals are man-made, the boats always remain in the market, and the goods are brought in via truck. This is necessary for the place to function, but only for it to function as a tourist site.

Culler (1981, p. 27) gives a very full explanation of this phenomenon:

> The tourist is not interested in the alibis a society uses to refunctionalize its practices. The tourist is interested in everything as a sign of itself, an instance of a cultural practice: a Frenchman is an example of a Frenchman, a restaurant on the Left Bank is an example of a Left-Bank-Restaurant: it signifies "Left-Bank-Restaurantness." All over the world the unsung armies of semiotics, the tourists, are fanning out in search of the signs of Frenchness, typical Italian behavior, exemplary Oriental scenes, typical American thruways, traditional English pubs; and, deaf to the natives' explanations that thruways are just the most efficient way to get from one place to another, or that pubs are just convenient places to meet your

> friends and have a drink, or that gondolas are the natural way to get around in a city full of canals, tourists persist in regarding these objects and practices as cultural signs.

A place removed from its organic function, from its native people, thus simply becomes sign of authenticity for us to consume.

Conclusion

Pseudo-authenticity consists of three domains, 1) that of the influence of media on our preconceptions of a culture, which thus influences are decoding of the signs and re-encoding through photography, 2) of the enjoyment we get from the fakery of the sites, and 3) our consumption of signs generate by the façades that permeate tourist attractions. Whereas Antirealism would validate these domains by claiming any authenticity they have is socially constructed by tourists, we instead argue that the tourist sites are beyond authenticity, that any authenticity we may perceive is instead signs of authenticity that are constructed to ensure we enjoy our experiences.

In the next three chapters, we will apply this theoretical framework to analyse the six tourist sites and better show how it can give us some deeper insight into how signs of authenticity are consumed by tourists.

3 Preservation

> People are nostalgic about old ways of life, and they want to relive them in the form of tourism, at least temporarily.
>
> (Chhabra *et al.* 2003, p. 705)

The conflict between the preservation of cultural heritage assets and the effect that transforming them into tourism products has on the assets is a fundamental conflict in contemporary tourism development. It is also a major trend that "countries developing their tourism have also sought to recreate the 'heritage' of the built environment even if this is of an epoch now denigrated" (Urry and Larson 2011, p. 137), and China is no exception.

Some efforts to mitigate this have taken place; for example, with the rapid development of digital technology we can 'digitally' protect traditional villages. This includes digital storage of relevant data including historical context and spatial data for architectural and road system design and creation of a digital museum full of digital products available on the internet (Su 2022). In this way, fragile tangible cultural assets can be protected, conserved, and available for consumption by digital tourists, and it removes many more barriers to access. However, this is not a long-term solution as this kind of digital archive tends to be removed from the tourism ecosystem as digital tourists do not need to pay for transportation, accommodation, and other amenities, thus providing no economic benefit.

As discussed in Chapter 2, while on the one hand some measure of transformation is needed, commodifying cultural assets for tourist consumption changes their role in a community and society and, thus, their meaning. On the other hand, the cultural asset will not be able to be safely and successfully accessed by tourists if efforts are not taken to develop it into a proper tourism product. The conflict between modernization and traditional ways of living becomes very apparent in the treatment of traditional villages in China. While many have been destroyed for the development of shopping malls or modern apartment buildings, many have been preserved and turned into heritage sites for domestic tourists. The objectives of cultural heritage management are

DOI: 10.4324/9781003291817-3

to "conserve a representative sample of our tangible and intangible heritage for future generations" (du Cros and McKercher 2015, p. 50). Saying that it should only be a 'representative sample' "acknowledges that not everything can or should be conserved, only the best or most representative of all that has gone before" (du Cros and McKercher 2015, p. 50).

Hou (2022) and Guo (2022) both look at the preservation of tourist resources in the context of the rural revitalization strategy. Hou (2022) discusses the dilemma of coordinated development of the rural tourism cultural industry and intangible cultural heritage protection, such as the dilemma between developing the tourist industry and protecting heritage assets, pointing out that often the prioritization of economic goals has led to homogenization and that the re-development of intangible culture has been ignored. Meng (2022) relates the preservation and tourist development of Gansu to the global context, arguing that such movement contributes to the inheritance, exchange, and research of world cultural heritage.

When considering which cultural heritage assets to preserve, several aspects need to be considered, such as "rarity, research or teaching potential, representativeness (is it a good example of its kind?), visual appeal, evidence of technical or innovative processes and associations with special individuals, cultural practices or spiritual beliefs" and the "importance of acknowledging something from all phases of historical development of many types of heritage assets . . . conserve and interpret the entire fabric of a place and not only its original structure" (du Cros and McKercher 2015, pp. 76–77). This requires conscious effort and centralized organization, yet the compromises reached and the need to convert assets to products, we will argue, causes the cultural products to be out of the domain of authenticity, simple signs of the assets they once were.

This chapter will look at two cases, Mt. Yunji in Xinfeng County and Huitong Village in Zhuhai. While it is certain that historical buildings and sites go through expensive renovations after their original purpose is finished in order to make them acceptable tourist sites (Staples 1995), Mt Yunji takes this to the extreme. The stones, brick, and wood from traditional villages in other provinces, such as Anhui and Hunan, have been transported there and re-constructed into a hybrid cultural preservation site and local 'theme park' located in a natural preservation zone. While it is certain that "purpose-built heritage products often function better as tourism attractions than extant assets" (du Cros and McKercher 2015, p. 113), Mt Yunji tries to thread the needle by being purpose-built using extant assets.

In the case of Huitong Village, the village has been affected by two aspects: the construction of a university nearby and its transformation into a local tourist site by the preservation of the old village and many of its buildings. Du Cros and McKercher note that "cultural heritage asset[s]" which are "recognized as being of high cultural significance" call for preservation "for future generations to observe and understand" (du Cros and McKercher 2015,

p. 50). Huitong Village is of much local cultural and historical significance, as evidenced by the renovations and preservation efforts made over the last 10 years.

Yet can we ascribe 'cultural significance' to the stones and wood from disassembled houses transported cross country and reassembled in the middle of a nature preserve? Re-purposing the materials is preferable to destroying them, but reconstruction primarily based on tangible assets without connection to intangible cultural assets is far separated from the traditional experience that tourists seek.

Reconstructed historical sites are outdoor museums, and, as Bruner notes, "like all museums, the way it is apprehended by the visitors is primarily visual" (Bruner 1994, p. 404). This is very true for the two sites under analysis, as the visual features of the sites have been the major source of improvement and consumer of resources. Huitong Village had extensive renovations to the 'wild' area around the village, including the creation of a well-landscaped park, the conversion of the muddy canal into a more idyllic flowing stream lined with rocks, construction of newer buildings in a mixed classical-modern design. Mt Yunji, on the other hand, almost seems designed to be in as many photos as possible, giving a sense of being some kind of fairyland where every tree, rock, and building is perfectly placed. At the same time, Huitong is not really an 'outdoor museum,' at least not as much as other preserved sites with a living culture, as the extant cultural practices are already modernized.

These cases form two sides of the same coin for cultural preservation and restoration and handle their nature as a tourist site in very different ways. Both must compromise authenticity to a major extent to facilitate tourism. Yet both are also increasingly common styles of cultural preservation in modern Chinese tourism, and thus, their relationship to authenticity can be an indication of future tourism development trends. They also present a good contrast to other historical preservation efforts around the world, and the implications for the development strategies for these two sites more universally will also be explored.

Huitong Village, Zhuhai

Located in Tangjiawan Town by the Phoenix Mountain in Xiangzhou District of northern Zhuhai, Huitong Village is a traditional Cantonese village mixed with Western architectural styles. It was listed as a district-level unit of cultural relic protection in 2006 and a provincial-level traditional village in 2014 (Local Chronicle Office of Guangdong Provincial People's Government 2019).

The village was initially constructed in 1732, the Qing Dynasty of Emperor Yongzheng. At the time, Mo Yujing purchased the land for the construction and had his fellows the Baos and the Tans moving here. For the generosity in his financial support, the villagers named the place after Mo

Huitong. In light of the Westernization Movement of the Qing Dynasty in the mid-nineteenth century, Huitong villagers went overseas including Hong Kong and Macau to seek their fortunes, with the three generations of the Mos (Mo Shiyang, Mo Zaoquan, and Mo Gansheng) working as agents for Swire, at the time the biggest British business organization in Hong Kong. With the wealth they amassed in Swire's shipping, sugar, insurance, and international trade business, they brought more than 1,000 people out of the country and created a management team that understood Western business practices. During the period of empires from Tongzhi to Guangxu of the Qing Dynasty, Huitong Village was rebuilt under unified planning with investment from wealthy overseas relatives at that time. The main buildings include two diaolou, three ancestral temples, and more than 40 residential buildings.

The development of Huitong Village went through three stages. The first phase was the reconstruction by successful businessmen in the mid-nineteenth century, which gave Huitong Village its most and main buildings that last till today. These buildings were constructed under a unified plan that brought modernization and Westernization to the village. The mix of traditional Chinese and Western styles was modelled after the Chinese concept of fengshui and Western concepts of modern town planning. Despite 170 years of political and economic ups and downs in modern China, Huitong Village still retains the unique style of the complete ancient village, which contains rich and precious architectural assets as well as cultural and historical connotations.

The transformation of Huitong Village's tangible and intangible cultural heritage assets into tourism products started in the second phase in around 2001. Its administrative area was reorganized to include it and three other nearby villages in Tangjiawan Town. From 2004 to 2005, the urban planning scheme of Tangjiawan New Town was developed, and the Institute of Urban Planning of Tongji University and the National Research Center of Historical and Cultural Cities were invited to jointly plan the preservation scheme of Tangjiawan's history and culture, among which Huitong Village is one of the special sites. Starting in 2015, the Gaoxin District of Zhuhai carried out comprehensive maintenance and revitalizing utilization of the gates, ancestral halls, and diaolou in Huitong. From 2015 to 2019, the government restored various buildings in the village and opened them to the public, transformed into, for example, a small cinema, a bookstore, and a history museum, including the restoration of the original British clock, which was imported over 100 years ago (Zhuhai National Hi-techIndustrial Development Zone 2020).

The third phase focused on the discursive construction of Huitong Village as a tourist attraction, which aimed to align with the national rural revitalization strategy. The rural revitalization strategy was proposed by President Xi Jinping in the Report of the 19th CPC National Congress in 2017 and initiated as one of the 5-year plans with the document Strategic Planning for Rural Revitalization (2018–2022) in September 2018 (The State Council 2018). It aims at the modernization of Chinese rural villages through the revitalization of their industries, talents, cultures, ecology, and institutionalization. Huitong Village is one of the projects in Zhuhai City which follows this national strategy. Through preservative measures including improving the infrastructure, promoting garbage sorting, excavating the cultural connotation of the village, and cooperating with the surrounding universities, Huitong Village was transformed into a key tourist site of Zhuhai under the project of rural revitalization. The transition met the general goals of the strategy by institutionalizing tourism, modernizing the infrastructures, and re-accommodating the local villagers.

Previous Studies

Research on Huitong village specifically is scarce. A 2016 survey of two cultural heritage sites in Zhuhai, including Huitong, showed the two most important "resource values" for the sites were "historic value" and "authenticity (retaining the traditional style)," followed by "aesthetic value" and "ambience or setting" (Yan *et al.* 2017, p. 362). However, at the time, Huitong Village was at a disadvantage to other such historical villages in Zhuhai, such as Jiexia Village, due to its relatively remote location and distance from other tourist sites (ibid). Since 2017 a lot of effort has gone into upgrading the facilities in Huitong, as noted earlier, including extensive landscaping, installation of parking lots and public toilets, construction of a tourist centre, and inclusion in the Zhuhai Green Line tourist route.

Xiao and Li (2022) analyse the renewal strategy of Huitong village with the concept of "co-governance and sharing" (18).

> By combining the characteristic cultural connotation of traditional villages with the local tourism industry, the supporting public service facilities can attract tourists and external capital investment, thus transforming the local industrial structure and stimulating the innovation vitality of the villages.
> (Xiao and Li 2022, p. 18)

The renovation included aspects of places for public activities, public service facilities, and residential architecture.

Aesthetic Analysis

As of 2019, there are 38 residential buildings remaining in Huitong Village, among which the most representative ones are the Mo Family Grand Ancestral Hall, built in Qing Dynasty, Jilu, the House of Mo Jiqing, built in 1934 by Mo Jiqing's son Mo Ru'en, and Qixiaxian Pavilion, a Western-style villa and garden built in 1918–1922 by Mo Yongru. In Mo Family Grand Ancestral Hall, the main building features three patios, a blue brick wall, grey tile

Figure 3.1 Photos from Huitong Village

surface, an ancient ridge, and a granite rock foundation, with decorations of brick, wood, and stone carving. Jilu contains a small two-story Western-style concrete building with a small courtyard in the middle, a pavilion on the roof, and exquisite European decoration inside. Qixiaxian Pavillion is a large garden-style hall with a gate building, an abstinence hall, a Guanyin pond, a hexagonal pavilion, a thatched pavilion, an artificial rock, and an electric generator room.

Huitong has two diaolou, or watchtowers, the one on the north is a four-story rectangle building and the one on the south is a two-and-a-half-storey circular arc building. Both were built during the period of the Republic of China and renovated in 2011. The watchtowers have lookout posts on their tops and gunports and windows all around for self-defence of the village during the warlord period. The *diaolou* style is a combination of defence and residence functions and blends the Chinese and Western architectural designs.

The village contains many shops, restaurants, and cafes to serve the tourists and nearby university students and staff. Several newer-style buildings were constructed to replace the ones demolished during the transformation process, ownership being given to villagers who were displaced to ensure they had a place to live and property to be developed to help the tourism infrastructure. Extensive landscaping transformed the green spaces into a more modern-style park, with paths and pavilions scattered about to allow for a leisurely stroll and many photo opportunities. The canals and rivers around the village were lined with stone to help both with flood control and to give a more aesthetically pleasing view. The stone streets were preserved and traffic was limited to those who reside in the village, with a parking lot outside for visitors. However, some building features were demolished to allow for cars to move through the village more freely, especially notable in the main *dialou* whose left archway was removed to give vehicles greater access to the back of the village.

Several features are targeted entirely at tourists, such as the tourist guide centre featuring Huitong-themed souvenirs, such as cups, notebooks, clothing such as t-shirts, and stamps. Pre-pandemic, there was also a costume shop, featuring a wide variety of ancient and classical-style outfits for tourists to rent to take photos. As with many similar well-preserved and maintained classical-style villages and neighbourhoods in China, Huitong is also used for wedding photography, with many wedding services listing Huitong as a possible venue. Concerts and performances can also be held in the village, from more modern rock music by students from the nearby universities or more classical performances of Chinese dance and music, although the schedule is irregular.

Review Analysis

Several reviews of Huitong Village were found on cTrip.com and only a few mentioned authenticity. In general, the tourists do not care so much about authenticity, but see it as a place with shops and peculiarities to relax. Some of the reviews did mention the historical facts of the village, with descriptions on the styles and characteristics of the architecture. Most importantly, it is its difference from modernity and metro life that gives people a sense of relaxation.

Three reviews remarked that the spot was good for leisure,

- "very suitable for leisure vacation" (Jiang, 2023–01–04).
- "a walk in the long old streets gives a calming feeling" (EDS, 2020–10–20).
- "allows a person in the hustle and bustle of the city to enjoy a quiet life" (Bo 2016–10–27)

Five praised the aesthetic feeling of the village:

- "the whole village is antique, tree-lined" (Jiang, 2023–01–04).
- "full of charming Lingnan residential buildings with neat layout, uniform appearance and color" (Qing, 2021–08–23).
- "some Lingnan architectural characteristics, black bricks, gray tile, cornices and other characteristics!" (Shang, 2017–02–19).
- "Ancient scenery, ancient color" (Bo 2016–10–27)
- "The scenery in the village is also OK, and there are a lot of longyan trees!"

(Shang, 2017–02–19)

Despite the efforts to make Huitong very photogenic, only one comment mentioned that it is "good for taking pictures" (Yu, 2018–02–19).

What the visitors are mainly concerned with is the environment, consuming signs of old-style buildings in please rural surroundings. But is a very sanitized rural village, one without poverty and deprivation, without struggle, where the *diaolou* watchtower is an object of photography, not a vital means of defence of the village from roaming bandits. It is an idealized version of the past with all the convenience of the present, made as an easy escape for urbanites in Zhuhai. The lack of intangible cultural elements, outside of the design of the buildings, seems to have little effect on tourists, as they are happy to consume the signs of the tangible products, the façades of the houses, Ancestral Hall, and the park.

Mt Yunji, Xinfeng

Rapoport (1984) defines three types of material elements, fixed, semi-fixed, and non-fixed. As Nuryanti defines it, "fixed elements" are "those that change only rarely and slowly and are organized and structured, such as buildings, towns and ruins" (Nuryanti 1996, p. 252). Yet, Mt Yunji does not fit into that category as it is reconstructed from a variety of 'fixed' elements into a new 'fixed' organized structure. The formerly 'fixed' tangible assets were changed very quickly and suddenly as the materials forming the buildings were disassembled and moved across China to a completely new area. Usually, it is smaller items like pottery or artefacts like jewellery that are considered as 'non-fixed,' yet in our case, entire villages have become unfixed in space and time and recontextualized.

Mt Yunji Ancient Village is a cultural heritage site built in the Mt Yunji National Reserve Park on the outskirts of Xinfeng County, north-east Guangdong Province. It was built out of already existing hillside villages in Anhui and Hunan which were disassembled piece by piece and reassembled in a purpose-built area in the national reserve park. This was done nominally to increase tourism to the park, which already featured hiking trails, restaurants, and spas. Mt Yunji belongs to the state, and in 2012, a development management contract was signed with Xinfeng Yunjishan Xuri Tourism Development Co., Ltd. (Re)construction of the ancient town was started in 2013 and continues to this day. According to promotional material, in 2017 the entire Mt Yunji Park received 210,000 tourists, with specific numbers for the Ancient Village not kept.

It is part of the Yunji Mountain cultural tourism development project, which includes other components such as hot springs, hotels, and commercial streets, integrative hiking trails, recreation, leisure, and sightseeing. The project is part of the Master Plan for Tourism Development in Xinfeng County (2017–2030) and is integrated into the county's Fourteenth Five-Year Plan of cultural tourism industry (Xinfeng County Bureau of Culture, Radio, Film, Tourism and Sports 2021a), in line with the national Fourteenth Five-Year Plan (2021–2025). The project includes the development of tourist sites scattered around Xinfeng County.

Yunji Old Town takes the development of unique ancient towns as the starting point and the collection of traditional dwellings of Ming and Qing Dynasties as the means, relocating and rebuilding ancient buildings throughout Jiangxi, Anhui, Fujian, and other provinces in China (Xinfeng County Bureau of Culture, Radio, Film, Tourism and Sports 2021b). All the buildings are taken apart brick by brick from their original locations and reconstructed under Yunji Mountain. As of 2021, it consists of 55 buildings from Jiangxi Province and Anhui Province, under an ongoing plan to eventually relocate 300 ancient buildings from those places where they are faced with a lack of proper preservation.

The Old Town currently includes large historical buildings – a Hui-style ancestral hall in the Xianfeng period of the Qing Dynasty, in the mid-1800s, and a large house of red bricks from Minnan area made in the Guangxu period of the Qing Dynasty, in the late 1800s. There are plenty of other buildings such as an opera stage, halls, and a wooden carving building (Xinfeng County Bureau of Culture, Radio, Film, Tourism and Sports 2021b).

Hui-style architecture, from the Huizhou area in modern Anhui and Jiangxi Province, is one of the most important genres of traditional Chinese architectural styles. It is the birthplace of the Hui merchants who dominated the Chinese business community for over 500 years during the Ming and Qing Dynasties. This style mostly uses wood as frames, bricks as walls, and carved stones for decoration, with large size of beam frames, showing a superb level of decorative art. With more than 40 main buildings having been built, the project intends to relocate 300 ancient buildings to provide rescue protection, systematization, and tourism development of traditional Chinese cultural resources.

According to workers at the site when we visited in 2017, more than 300 buildings will "come together" at the foothills of Yunji Mountain from 2018 to 2019. At present, the construction team of 50 to 60 people are working continuously, and the historical and cultural excavation behind it is proceeding simultaneously. As of 2021, there are 35 ancient buildings under construction, of which ten have been completed with the main and exterior decoration, five are undergoing internal renovation, and several other styles of buildings will also be completed in batches in the future

Aesthetic Analysis

First, you have to drive up a winding road from the small city of Xinfeng below. On the way up you see not only other cars but couples on motorcycles. This seems very odd at first as the road is very steep and takes a good half-hour in a proper car; the voyage by such small motorcycles must take an hour.

Once you get to the site, and before you park, the first site to catch your eye are two giant wooden water wheels. They are suspended above a small stream reinforced with rocks and are immobile because the stream is not strong enough to push the wheels. They are also not connected to anything, such as a mill or other mechanical device. What more ultimate indication of the completely symbolic nature of the site is needed than immovable wheels?

Figure 3.2 Photos from Mt. Yunji

After parking, you cross under the main archway and enter the apparent 'main street' and are instantly impressed by the beauty of the buildings; wooden supports made of single trees that still have the nubs where the branches were cut off, unfinished, unvarnished, unpainted; intricate wooden latticework on the balconies and windows and doors; bats and lotuses and phoenixes carved into wooden and stone plaques above doorways and archways; the sloping tiled rooves curve upwards and are capped off by koi; the unevenly shaped bricks that make up the walls. There is obviously a mix of old and new here indicated by the level of wear on the stone and wood. Some woodwork is older and greyer and dingy; some is fresh, sharp brown. Some carvings are weathered by time; some, sharp and discrete. The misshapen stone brickwork is held together by perfectly edged mortar. Some characters are so eroded that you can barely make them distinct, while the main archway's stonework is so fresh it could be seen anywhere in modern China.

Then you come across what appears to be several shops, as indicated by banners saying 'tea' and 'XXX.' Yet most shops are empty, even several years after the site opened. One shop space was eventually populated, selling jade and gold jewellery, umbrellas, and ice cream. The banners outside the shops are made of a single rustic bamboo rod attached to the overhand with rough cotton string, yet the banner itself is printed, cut, and shaped by machine, capped by the modern name "Mt. Yunji," instead of being hand-painted.

In the middle of the reconstructed town, you are greeted by an idyllic pond encircled by several giant rocks, above it on the hill is another striking traditional building partially hidden behind the bamboo trees. Here you find that if you want to cross the steam bisecting the site you have to cross over a rock path bridge.

The ancient buildings mainly include five styles: Anhui Huizhou Architecture, Minnan Red Brick Traditional Residence, Guangfu Architecture, Ganlan Style Folk House, and Hakka Weilong House. Huizhou Architecture was mainly acquired in Anhui, Jiangxi, and Zhejiang provinces, especially the ancient Huizhou. In the region, the Red Brick Traditional Residence mainly comes from buildings such as Xiamen, Zhangzhou, and Quanzhou in Fujian Province. The Hakka Wei Building mainly comes from the junction of Guangdong and Jiangxi. Guangfu Building was acquired in the Pearl River Delta region. Ganlan-style buildings are mostly from the Nanling Range. All the buildings were acquired on the original site.

Interview Analysis

But what of the people who visit the site? They are mainly families, extended families visiting Xinfeng during holidays brought by their local relatives or nuclear families visiting during normal times. The site also attracts wedding photography.

Three respondents were local families who came as an activity with their children, while three others came to bring their friends. The site itself seems to be just another place to go for them, YJ5 noting "I think the environment is very comfortable" and JY4 noting they brought their kids "to play in the stream."

Two of the respondents mentioned they thought the site was quite authentic: "I think it's very authentic. They are all historical and tore apart and brought here" (YJ1) and "Authentic. Very vintage, antique and classical beauty" (YJ2).

Three had a more negotiated position, with one praising the 'copy': "I think it's done a good job in copying because it's quite vintage" (YJ3). Two others could only comment on the outward façade of the site, how it 'looks,' saying "The buildings and the outside are not bad. The style looks vintage" (YJ5). However, they were also quite critical, saying the "authenticity is just so-so. Not very classical since you can tell it's new" (YJ6).

They also made direct comparisons to Anhui, which was the source of most of the buildings at that stage of the project: "The style looks like Anhui" (YJ6) and "I don't know how it was in Anhui but I think it's done a good job" (YJ3).

Two additional ones admitted they could not judge the authenticity "It's beautiful but I don't know how authentic it is since I have never seen the real one" (YJ4) and "I don't know the ancient time but this looks ok" (YJ7).

The motivations for the tourists to visit had to do more with finding something to do to pass the time with friends, or a place to bring children, "Brought kids to play in the stream" (JY4) and "bring kids here every summer" (JY7).

The main complaint was that the site was still being developed, with four respondents mentioning that. All in all the respondents were more concerned with the outward façade of the site giving signs of classical and ancient times. The site still lives in a direct relationship to its referent, its style being cross-referenced to 'Anhui' even if the respondent knew about the Anhui style or not.

Reviews Analysis

Reviews of Mt. Yunji online were nearly impossible to find. Only one from 2020 was found on cTrip.com:

> At the foot of Yunji Mountain, there is Yunji Mountain Ancient Street, which gathers ancient buildings from all over the country, such as exquisite wooden buildings, small bridges and flowing water, and ancient streets. Not many tourists come to visit here, which is very quiet and suitable for taking photos here. There are also many professional photography teams in period costumes to shoot here. The combination of ancient buildings and nature is refreshing.

Yet in this single review, we can see many of the aspects of pseudo-authenticity; the inherent photogenic qualities of the site and the 'refreshing' experience one can have there. Similar to Huitong, the authenticity of Mt Yunji is not what tourists see as the most important. They are fine to consume the signs of ancient culture, the tangible assets converted to façades of old-style buildings in an idyllic mountain scene.

Yet do the developers put so much effort into their re-creations only for the tourists to not appreciate it? Why not simply create new buildings in the old style from scratch using modern materials instead of transporting fragile brick and wood across China and painstakingly restore and reconstruct it? Because then the site would not be special or notable. The recycling of old materials to preserve the past is what creates the uniqueness and meaning of the site. More importantly, it gives the visitors an alibi for their journey.

Conclusion

Effect of Media

The popularity of historical dramas and knowledge passed down through education and history of China is a strong motivator to travel to such sites, especially as the tourists can take photos to share on their social media. Huitong Village, as mentioned, also has historical clothing rental shops to assist in tourists creating that special, sharable moment. Rentals of such historical clothing are popular at sites all around China, including in Hangzhou's West Lake and Beijing's Forbidden City. Even in certain places outside China dressing up in period costumes is an important ritual for young tourists, like how the influence of Korean dramas in China has led to the growth of such rental shops around Seoul's Gyeongbokgung Palace and other classic buildings. This allows for the proliferation of signs of history and antiqueness, learned through school but mostly through media.

More importantly, idealized views of the purity and simplicity of the past allow these sites to become refugees for urban folk looking to escape the big city. While it is certain that tourists "are nostalgic about old ways of life, and they want to relive them in the form of tourism, at least temporarily" (Chhabra *et al.* 2003, p. 705), the extent to which it can be temporarily 'relived' is questionable. One can wander around the site and take photos and enjoy the scenery, yet that is not what people in the olden days did. We can sit in a modern restaurant and eat a meal with our friends and colleagues, yet the food we consume is modernized, and the conveniences (AC, lighting, Wi-Fi, hot water) are modern. We relive in a shallow way that still keeps us in our bubble of modernity. We can travel to any non-urban place to get away from it all, but the added benefit of these kinds of preserved (and reconstructed) sites is they are closer to urban areas and also tend to feature parks and a constructed 'natural' environment around the restored buildings.

Façadism

Mt Yunji differs from Huitong village in regard to façadism as Mt Yunji *only* contains facades and there are literally no locals or original intangible culture that could be transformed into products. The site is purely consumed for the images of the old buildings in an idyllic setting up in the hills. There is no history to contend with and not even any intangible culture to be corrupted by commercialism. It is pure tangible cultural assets, bricks and wood decontextualized from their original context and reconstituted in a theme park.

Huitong Village is more of a typical model of the preservation of an extent cultural site, with the construction of increased infrastructure and beautification efforts. The result, however, is that the majority of the locals from Huitong have moved away, leaving the facades of the village's buildings behind to be filled by restaurants and cafes and other amenities needed by the tourists (as well as teachers and students from the nearby university). The main local cultural assets that can be commodified are the architecture style and flower tea.

The Huitong village relies largely on its historical importance as a strong village during the turn of the century and the warlord period in Guangzhou. The presence of the two *diaolou*, although not as impressive as others such as in Kaiping, and the ancestral hall, although only for a marginally famous local historical figure, are the alibi for its preservation. The past is presented either as being from an obsolete, bygone era, or part of a national myth, and in this case, Huitong fulfils both roles.

Both sites give signs of classical China but in a highly sanitized manner, liberated from the presence of locals and beautified to standards far higher than similar existing classical villages. One can find thousands of similar villages in China from the same era which are living cultural assets not (yet) transformed into tourism products, but those kinds of villages feature locals living their life, full of intangible culture, yet with under-developed transportation infrastructure and a lack of systematic beautification efforts. But those kinds of villages are not suitable for tourism, and so places like Huitong are chosen to be representatives of classical villages for tourists to consume, facades of an antique era hollowed out of antiquated culture.

Authentic Fakery

This aspect is less present in these sites than in the other four in our study. Huitong Village itself is not consumed for its fakery, at least to a far less extent than Mt Yunji, because it is an actual preserved ancient village, although with extensive modifications to make it a consumable tourism product. It is better to say that people enjoy it for its façades and the sanitized signs of ancient villages than its fakery.

Mt. Yunji, on the other hand, is enjoyed for its uniqueness as a reconstructed site. It is more perfect than actual existing un-developed ancient villages because it is untarnished by actual people living their lives and actual organic development. It is completely reliant on pseudo-authenticity as the cultural products up for consumption are pure floating signs detached from any prerequisite cultural asset. According to their development plans, additional features will be added in the future, such as more shops and cultural shows, but those intangible cultural performances would still be completely detached from the intangible culture of the tangible assets as they have no context, no locals, and no place.

4 Miniaturization

Tourist attractions featuring the miniaturization of famous attractions are becoming a growing trend around the world, including sites such as Legoland parks in the US and UK, Swissminiatur in Switzerland, and Cockington Green Gardens in Australia. Splendid China and Window of the World, located in the Overseas Chinese Town district of Shenzhen, follow this trend and will be the focus of this chapter as they represent, on one hand, a kind of nation-building tourism that is growing rapidly around China, and on the other hand an increased interest and knowledge of global culture and tourism. Splendid China consists of miniature representations of extant and destroyed natural and built cultural sites of Greater China, both of the Han ethnic majority and various minority ethnic groups. The sister site, Window of the World, contains reproductions of famous tourist sites around the world. These kinds of sites are inspired by the World Expos of the turn of the century, in that instead of "tourists having to travel worldwide to experience and gaze upon different signs, they are conveniently brought together in one location" (Urry and Larson 2011, p. 133).

The original intention of their construction in the 1990s was part of the modernization of Shenzhen, to give the city more cultural content to promote tourism so that the economy was not too dependent on a single industry, the booming tech sector. Furthermore, as it was difficult for most Chinese to travel abroad to see world-famous sites, Window of the World was able to bring them together in one location. Splendid China, on the other hand, is part of a nation-building process, codifying what exactly, out of the thousands of cultural assets around China, are the most representative of China, including both from across different dynasties and from the various ethnic groups which make up modern China.

This gives these sites a much more fraught relationship with authenticity; They are even more obviously far away from the original sites due to their miniature nature, yet it does give one a sense of the diversity of styles and cultures of the world by allowing tourists to consume their signs and revel in the fakery. In many ways, this is similar to efforts at preservation of fragile cultural assets which cannot easily be adaptable to mass tourism (see Brooks

DOI: 10.4324/9781003291817-4

1993), yet with the added dimension of miniaturization to allow for a much greater quantity of assets to be displayed.

This is also common in themed shopping malls. Urry and Larson give the example of the West Edmonton Mall in Alberta, Canada, which "represents a symbolic rejection of the normally understood world geography in which there are cultural centers with Edmonton located upon the world's periphery" (Urry and Larson 2011, p. 128). Instead, Edmonton is centred with signs of global culture circulating in the city instead. Trafford Centre in Manchester, UK, is another example, with "a new collective sense of place based on transcending the barriers of distance and of place" (Urry and Larson 2011, p. 129).

Terminal 21 in Bangkok, Thailand, takes a slightly different approach, with the entire mall themed like an airport and each floor a different 'gate' bringing you around the world. Floors are themed after San Francisco, Rome, London, Istanbul, Japan, and the Caribbean, with the prerequisite decorations giving signs of the original locations. This includes street signs, statues, a restaurant located in a replica San Francisco Cable Car, a miniature Golden Gate Bridge suspended over the escalators, a clothing shop in a double-decker London bus replica, Thai souvenirs sold in a variety of small shops underneath an impressive display of Turkish-style lanterns, and on and on. Yet each floor is themed in the way a normal mall is, the top floors for restaurants, two for women's clothing and makeup, one for men's clothing, etc. In the competition for new designs for shopping malls to serve locals and tourists in central Bangkok, Terminal 21's design is a pure spectacle and signs of famous tourist sites, a self-referential playground and a must-see for travellers to Bangkok.

Outline of Sites

The Window of the World is a cultural theme park that opened in June 1994. According to its website, it includes "more than 130 places of historic interest and scenic beauty, the ethnic customs performance in the whole world, showing the essence and cultures from different countries as well as the exotic folk customs" while also bringing "the dynamic trend and the most rich and colorful 'World tour' to tourists with more stylish entertainment elements" (Shijiezhichuang 2023). It features a mix of miniature replicas of famous buildings, temples, towers, statues, and natural sites from around the world, as well as cultural dance and musical performances.

Next to the Window of the World is Splendid China Folk Village, an ethnic and heritage theme park based similarly on miniatures of famous temples and buildings from China, founded in 1990. This is China in a very broad sense, including not only Mainland China but also Hong Kong, Macau, and Taiwan, as well as various ethnic minority sites from around Greater China, thus constructing China in a multi-ethnic manner, albeit one in which the different Chinese cultures are segregated, with Han Chinese culture given as 'normal' and the cultures of the various minority groups as 'ethnic.'

Both sites are run by the Shenzhen Jinxiu China Development Co., Ltd., established in 1988 by the China Travel Service (HK) Group Corporation and Shenzhen Overseas Chinese Town Group. Both parks are located in Overseas Chinese Town in the Nanshan District of Shenzhen, a special economic zone in Southern China across the border from Hong Kong. Both sites are parts of the OCT Group's construction of an Overseas Chinese Town tourist attractions series in the city: Window of the World was established in 1994 and Splendid China in 1989. The fact that both tourist sites were built by commercial tourist companies makes it less implicit that the operation of the theme parks is intrinsically commercialized cultural products. Overseas Chines Town Enterprises, founded in 1985, runs other theme park franchises across China, such as eight "Happy Valley" theme parks, which are more general ride-based parks. One subsidiary is Overseas Chinese Town Limited, which in partnership with China Travel Service (Hong Kong), runs two Window of the World Parks, one in Shenzhen, Guangdong, and one in Changsha, Hunan.

The sister site, Window of the World, contains reproductions of famous tourist sites around the world. This gives these sites a much more fraught relationship with authenticity. They are even more obviously far away from the original sites due to their miniature nature, yet it does give one a sense of the diversity of styles and cultures of the world. By 2014, Window of the World has welcomed 55 million tourists from around the world while Splendid China has received around 60 million tourists from home and abroad (Splendid China, n.d.).

Window of the World

Aesthetic Analysis

The park is remarkably large, covering an area of 480,000 square meters. It contains more than 130 attractions, including replicas of the Eiffel Tower, the Taj Mahal, the Pyramids of Giza, and the Statue of Liberty. The park is divided into nine zones, each representing a different region or continent. The zones are connected by a monorail system that runs through the park, and electric carts can also be rented.

Each zone has its own architectural style, landscape design, and cultural features. For example, the European zone has a classical and romantic atmosphere, with fountains, statues, and gardens. The Asian zone has a diverse and exotic flair, with temples, pagodas, and bamboo forests. The African zone has a wild and adventurous vibe, with savannahs, waterfalls, and wildlife.

The park also offers various performances and shows that reflect the customs and traditions of different countries. For example, visitors can watch a flamenco dance from Spain, African dances, or a carnival parade in Brazil. The park also hosts festivals and events throughout the year, such as Oktoberfest

Figure 4.1 Photos from Window of the World

and a Halloween party. There are several activities as well, such as an Alps-themed ice skating rink under a replica of the Matterhorn, camel rides by the Sphinx and Pyramids. Costume shops abound, renting out such a wide variety of stereotypical clothing from Europe, Africa, and Asia.

The miniatures are all of wildly different scales, so it is hard to generalize. The Eiffel Tower replica is a 1/3 scale replica, while the Arc de Triomphe is around half the original size. The UK Parliament Building is around 10 meters tall, yet has extensive details for the windows, roof, and brickwork. It is placed along a small stream and is neighboured by a replica of the Tower Bridge which crosses that stream. There is a replica of the Palace in Versailles, including a miniature of the gardens created with real plants and working miniature fountains.

Under the Eiffel Tower replica is a stage where performers occasionally come out to do different styles of dance. On our visit, the dancer, an internationally diverse group of a mix of nationalities, even came out into the crowd to dance with the visitors and eventually started a conga line.

One has to climb upstairs to get to the top of the tower, where there are good views of the rest of the park; you can even rent a small telescope to have a closer look around the park from the high vantage point. There are also several vendors, selling ice cream, soda, and other snacks, as well as typical offerings at Chinese tourist sites, such as plastic gourd whistles, bouncing balls, and other toys for kids, and paintbrushes, jade necklaces, and stone bracelets for adults. You can even get your name carved on a traditional Chinese-style stone stamp on the spot.

We could go on to describe more and more details of the miniatures and arrangement of the park; however, the main point is that it is a chaotic amalgamation of famous buildings and landscapes. If you change your perspective slightly, you can see both Big Ben and the Eiffel Tower in the same view. From the right angle, you can capture lower Manhattan, the Capitol Building, the Washington Monument, the Lincoln Monument, the Statue of Liberty, and Mt Rushmore in the same shot. Geography, scale, time, and space all disappear as we are confronted by a never-ending deluge of signs of famous places, some which we know very well and might have even travelled to, and others which we can 'see' for the first time.

Interview Analysis

The main motivation for visiting WW is that the site itself is a famous tourist attraction in Shenzhen, with ten respondents noting this to varying degrees. WW15 noted that it was highly ranked when searching online for sites in Shenzhen, while five others heard from word-of-mouth. WW4 noted that it is the "must-go place in Shenzhen," while WW6 noted that it is a "landmark" of the city.

Secondarily, tourists were motivated to come to WW because they wanted to "kill time" as something to do with their friends, with four respondents directly stating that. An additional three said they wanted to come just to "have a look" or that they were "curious." WW20, interestingly, noted they came simply because "there's nothing else to see in Shenzhen," while WW1 noted they only came to "take some pictures."

Few of the interviewees praised the authenticity of the site, saying the attractions look "real, authentic" (WW2) or "distinctive and authentic" (WW6). "It's authentic, very delicate, splendid. Makes me feel like I'm right there" (WW19).

Others admitted they cannot judge the authenticity because they haven't seen the real places:

- "They look real, even though I haven't been to the real one" (WW18)
- "Never been to the real ones so no idea" (WW3)
- "I don't know about authenticity, I've never seen the real ones" (WW4)
- "Kinda real. Never seen before"

(WW6)

One related it to their previous experience, that "It's like what's told in history books" (WW18). Another seemed to be doing research, saying they came "to have a look first so as to know about it. I plan on going to some of them later" (WW6).

Tourists were encountered from around China, and most were critical of the authenticity.

- "So-so, not very real, but comfortable and fresh" (WW8).
- "Buildings are not bad, not very real" (WW10).
- "Some are ok but doesn't have any human touch" (WW11).
- "Not authentic. I studied Construction. Not very delicate" (WW16).
- "Some look real, so do not."

(WW17)

Another theme was the gap between their anticipation and the advertising and their actual experience:

- "it's not as amazing as advertised" (WW20).
- "not as interesting as imagined. Not very real" (WW12).
- "Not as good as I imagined, very fake, not very fake but *very very* fake. Expect for the Eifel Tower [Replica]."

(WW15)

Two of the interviewees were foreign tourists, one from India and one from Russia, and neither visited for the sake of authenticity. WW9 saying they went "just to kill time" and WW5 saying "authenticity isn't very important, just a place to hang out at" as he was visiting a friend working in Shenzhen. For Chinese, it was the same, five only went to 'kill time,' three because of the lack of other touristy things to do in Shenzhen, and three because they were visiting friends in the city. One admitted the only reason they came was to "take some pictures" (WW1).

Interestingly, six in total admonished the site's attractions for being 'too small,' while six others mentioned the site needed some repair as many of the attractions were worn out.

Review Analysis

As the site is quite famous and well-travelled, many reviews were found on both cTrip.com and TripAdvisor.

cTrip

Rarely had visitors discussed about the miniatures' authenticity. They mostly focused on their experience of taking photos, watching firework shows, watching performances by foreigners, hanging out with families, and doing the rides. They did comment on how the miniatures are old, delicate, and in need of repair.

- "the building is mini version, so lovely" (Ty811, 2023–03–20)
- "some miniaturization is excessive" (Yan, 2023–01–23)
- "The Eiffel Tower and Arc de Triomphe are relatively large, other buildings are very small" (E42, 2023–01–23)
- "There are many miniature landscapes in various countries" (Li, 2023–01–29)
- Two commented simply on the site containing famous buildings and attractions
- "There are all the world's major famous scenic spots" (Yan, 2023–01–23)
- "Super beautiful . . . the world's famous buildings"

(Ping, 2023–01–23)

One interesting comment implied that Window of the World was out of date:

> In the early days, people could not go abroad. These kinds of miniature scenic spot were still very marketable. Later, with the development of economy, I can go abroad to see the real thing, then why do I have to see the small ones?
>
> (Xibingwei, 2023–03–02)

TripAdvisor

The number of reviews was not very high, over 2000 in total; 24 were analysed in total, stopping after they became repetitive and saturation was reached.

Many reviews did not add any caveats about the authenticity of the miniature reproductions, using a very objective modality in their descriptions, using 'window,' 'introduction,' or 'insight' to describe the mode of viewing offered.

- "shows you lots of **significant landmark**s from around the world" (WW5–2021)
- "Tour the **highlight** [sic] **attractions** of the world" (WW6–2020)
- "a tour of the **world's famous** monuments" (WW9–2019a)
- "a real **window** to see the different parts of the world, Asian, European, American, African countries are represented in a way @ this park" (WW11–2019a)
- "introduces you to the world's **iconic sculptures and icons**. . . . It's is great experience to see the whole world compressed in a park" (WW12–2019e)
- "The attractions are very well made and offer genuine insight to **worldly attractions**"

(WW8–2020)

Others were more aware of the nature of the park and used a variety of expressions, such as 'recreation,' 'reproduction,' 'model,' or 'replica':

- "It was fun seeing miniature **recreations** of famous landmarks around the world" (WW7–2020)
- "interesting park with **reproductions** that are very impressive" (WW11–2019b)
- "offers **replica/models** of buildings and landmarks from across the world" (WW4–2019b)
- "A few **replica's** [sic] were pretty good but not all" (WW6–2019a)
- "It's a park with **Replica** attractions from different countries" (WW6–2019c)
- "it is quite amazing to see excellent **replicas** of the famous places in the world" (WW12–2019c)
- "you can see **flashes** from different & famous places in world.. such as Africa, Europe, Latin America & Asia"

(WW9–2019 b)

Only three in total mentioned the miniature nature of the attractions, showing they accept and appreciate the fakery provided in the park.

- "Some of the **miniature** have very minute details as well captured to perfection" (WW12–2019b)
- "You will find all the best places of the world gathered in one place, **miniaturized**" (WW11–2018)
- "The miniature replicas are awesome"

(WW6–2020)

Three reviewers more directly related the attractions to actually travelling abroad to see them. One respondent compared the miniatures to their own travel experiences and seemed to enjoy the fakery on play: "As a traveller having seen some of the great monuments and structures of the World it was great to 'see them again!'. They looked quite authentic" (WW4–2019c). Conversely, one stated that "It's interesting – probably more so for people who haven't had the opportunity to travel to see the things in real life" (WW4–2019b). The last implied that this kind of park is likely now obsolete: "This was probably something for folks who hardly get a chance to travel in the 90s or 2000s. But now, most people would have the opportunity to travel to see the real thing" (WW12–2019d).

The photogenic nature of the park was only mentioned by two reviewers, but both seemed to view it as a large part of the experience:

- "Be sure that you clear your memory cards, as there will be tons of photo-ops" (WW12–2019a)
- "I went twice and took hundred photos"

(WW12–2017)

Finally, the usefulness of the park for educating children was mentioned by three:

- "This place is a great way to get your child excited about traveling" (WW5–2021)
- "My kids and I enjoyed our afternoon here" (WW6–2019b)
- "Kids! You must go and set your future destination"

(WW12–2019e)

Conversely, one criticized the park for its state of disrepair and the negative effect this would have on children: "Most 'attractions' looked aged and some in ruins. In desperate need of a full revamp to stay relevant. Even kids may have a wrong concept of the 'world' in broken pieces" (WW5–2019).

Splendid China

Aesthetic Analysis

Much of what could be said here was said earlier when describing Window of the World. The main difference is that a lot more care seems to be taking place with the replications and their physical arrangement. Most individual buildings get their own separate area and do not feature in some sort of chaotic collage.

As mentioned in the introduction, the selection of which buildings to feature is a part of building up the image of the Chinese nation-state. Selections from all over the country are included, from the Portola Palace in Tibet, to the Great Wall in the north, to the Longmen Grottos from Luoyang in central China, to the Stone Forrest in Sichuan in the south-east, and to Hakka tulou from the east. They are integrated very well into the landscape, replicating not only the building but the environment around it. For example, the replica Mazu Temple from Fijian is built into the hillside, with the main pagoda on the top with the entryway at the bottom.

Unlike Window of the World, there are no modern buildings or other structures represented, it is all from ancient and classical China. The opportunity is even taken to re-create historical buildings that have been destroyed, such as the Summer Palace complex in Beijing that was demolished during the Boxer Rebellion by European powers. All of the buildings in the palace are reconstructed in great detail and arranged in the identical formation as they were originally.

Interview Analysis

For SC, the motivations were more mixed. Again, the highest proportion (four of eleven) came because of the famousness of the site. Secondarily, three came to "kill time" with friends or family. The remainder gave varying reasons,

Figure 4.2 Photos from Splendid China

from SC10 noting there were discounted tickets for that day, SC1 had come as part of a work trip, and SC5 noting that a search engine recommended it.

As with Window of the World, interviewees lightly praised the authenticity, saying it is "ok" (SC1, SC5), "just so-so" (SC8), or "kind of real" (SC4). One even praised the "The imitation is relatively successful, Very vivid" (SC9). Two were more entirely negative, saying because they replicas are "delicate" they "don't feel it's authentic" (SC11), and that the whole site "does not amaze me" (SC5). Three mentioned the size in a negative way, for example, one saying "If it's bigger then it looks more real" (SC6).

One interesting theme is the relationship of the miniatures to the real places, with several mentioning it has inspired them to go to the real places, "Maybe will go to the real one after seeing this" (SC7), or "Can't go to the real places so I came here" (SC4). Or at least educates them, "makes me familiar with Chinese culture and buildings" (SC5), while another felt they were authentic because "they are exactly the same as the real one I saw, expect for the size" (SC8).

Others, like with Window of the World, mention they cannot judge authenticity because they haven't been to the real ones "Haven't been to the others so don't know. But I can imagine how splendid they are by watching this" (SC3). "Haven't been to the real places so we don't have any special feelings here from them" (SC2).

Another admitted they were inspired by seeing images of the originals in the media: "I saw some on TV [before] but today I'm here to see them" (SC1).

Review Analysis

Reviews were found on both cTrip.com and TripAdvisor and were scoured for mentions of authenticity. cTrip mentions more about the sites' ability to allow the visitor to travel all around China in a short time, some also praising the educational value, especially for ethnic minority culture.

cTrip.com

One related the site more to China and the construction of national identity, saying it is "a miniature version of our great rivers and mountains and all kinds of famous buildings, in one day to enjoy the great rivers and mountains of the motherland" (hi, 2017–08–23).

One talks about it more in terms of efficiency, "I can visit all kinds of scenic spots and historic sites of the Chinese nation at one time" (Niu, 2019–11–16). While another related more to the educational: "learn more about the history and culture, as well as the local customs and customs of different regions" (Moka, 2016–09–14).

Two related the site to their previous and future travel plans: "I can also see where I have traveled and what places I have not been to" (Niu, 2019–11–16). "You can feel its elegance in many places that you have not been to" (Moka, 2016–09–14).

Two had differing opinions on the effect of the miniatures, one stating "Although they are all micro landscapes, I still feel very good" (Niu, 2019–11–16), while another stated "The views in the miniature area are just so-so" (Xiang, 2016–01–15).

TripAdvisor

Twenty-eight of the 1,200 reviews were examined, stopping after saturation was reached as before. Four focused on the diversity of the site and the representation of different ethnic groups in China, using verbs such as 'see,' 'view,' and 'visit':

- "see a lot of different cultures of China here" (SC1–2019)
- "see what living with each cultural minority would be like as well as see clothing, their culture, and religion" (SC3–2019)
- "fascinating view of China's cultural and racial diversity" (SC2–2019b)
- "visit different ethnic minority areas"

(SC2–2019a)

Three discussed it more in terms of the 'best,' 'great,' 'important,' 'famous,' and 'popular' tourist sites being replicated in the park:

- "all the **best places** to visit in China in just one huge area" (SC4–2019c)
- "the **most popular and interesting** places in China" (SC8–2019c)
- "you would be able to explore some of the **best tourist spots** of China" (SC12–2018b)
- "All the **most important** Chinese temples and palaces" (SC4–2019c)
- "all the **great places** in China (SC7–2019c)
- "**famous** sites"

(SC8–2019d)

Others focused on the scope of the site, some noting the shallowness and lack of depth, that it can only give an 'overview,' 'image,' 'glimpse,' or 'insight':

- "an overall idea/image of the various Chinese culture" (SC7–2019b)
- "an overview of the different regions and cultures within China" (SC11–2018)
- "a glimpse of the life of the minority ethnic groups of China" (SC8–2019d)
- "gives you insight of the many historic sites around China"

(SC12–2018d)

Others discussed it more positively, saying 'vast' or 'whole' to indicate the breadth of the site is more acceptable:

- "You can witness the **entire vast** provinces of China in one place" (SC6–2019b)
- "eye opener to China's **vast** tribes and religion" (SC8–2019b)
- "its like seeing **the whole of China** in one place"

(SC12–2019)

One review was more practical in nature, noting the site is good if your time in China is limited: "The miniatures are fun to watch if you, like us, only have a five-day visa and no time to explore entire China" (SC12–2018c).

The educational nature of the park was highlighted by quite a few reviewers,

- "learning more about the Chinese Culture" (SC3–2019)
- "learn and see the China minority tribes and buildings" (SC12–2018d)
- "learn about China . . . a quick lesson about the different cultures" (SC4–2019b)
- "understand more about different ethnic cultures of China" (SC2–2019a)
- "discover more about China" (SC7–2019c)
- "educational trip" (SC8–2019b)

- "teach [kids] and let them discover all the variety of China" (SC2–2019b)
- "know lots about the country and peak into many of its signature architecture and cultures" (SC12–2019)
- "educational . . . immersed in the myriad cultures of minority tribes from all over China"

(SC12–2018a)

Many more commented on the miniature nature of the park, with many praising the effort and effect: "**miniaturized** in a very meticulous way. Most of them look impressive" (SC4–2019c), "The miniatures are fun to watch" (SC12–2018c). One goes into more detail, calling it a "**tiny sculpture** town" which is "really worth seeing," specifically noting the "**miniature** Great Wall with its soldiers the forbidden city" pointing out "all its characters" (SC7–201a), meaning the tiny figurines of soldiers, horses, and other items affixed near the replica. Two called it "a mini [China]" (SC6–2019b), "like a mini-China" (SC11–2019), as, indeed, the replicas are geographically arranged in a slightly distorted map of China.

Finally, other than noting their 'miniature' nature, posters commented on the form and quality of the attractions at the site:

- "many good **replicas** . . . a good place to visualize what they are like" (SC8–2019d)
- "fairly **well designed**, with concrete (no plastic), correct painting, etc, including a few water flows to **mimic** rivers or cascades" (SC2–2019b)
- "**authentic rebuild** [sic] buildings" (SC7–2019c)
- "**superbly** [sic] and I would think **authentically designed**"

(SC10–2019)

One longer comment is quite interesting, as the reviewer relates it to their own living and travel experiences: "Having lived in Beijing for 3 years and toured around a bit we were **impressed with the accuracy and intricacy** of Forbidden city, heavenly and summer palaces models etc . . . the Great Wall model is Cecile B De Mille epic" (SC2–2021).

The final comment, which is very honest, simply states that Splendid China is "a cheesy park" (SC4–2019b), yet one poster still says they enjoy it.

Conclusion

Effect of Media

The omnipresence of world-famous attractions like the Eiffel Tower, Big Ben, the Pyramids, and the Great Wall of China, across the media, ensures that there is something for everyone at Window of the World and Splendid China.

No matter how educated or well-travelled you are, there is at least something that would draw you here and something you would recognize.

Reviews and interviews showed the visitors were mostly impressed because the attractions were famous places. So the Eiffel Tower is famous for being famous, and the replica of Window of the World is famous for being a famous copy of an attraction that is famous for being famous. The reason for coming to the site and the tourists' decoding process is entirely self-referential.

The photogenic quality of the sites also serves to guide tourists' gaze to find the perfect angle to capture the miniature. And it can be done in two styles as well, one which ignores the small size of the replica and tried to capture it as if it was the original, and one which emphasizes the miniature-ness by including a person in the shot, thus showing the true scale.

This is a true place of pseudo-authenticity. Certainly, these kinds of places existed a century ago in the form of exhibitions and World Fairs showing off cultures around the world, those expos were made by people from those cultures who would themselves travel to the expo to show off their own culture. They were of higher quality and temporary.

We should instead view these kinds of sites as products of modernization itself, of the spread of media content, both fictional and non-fictional, depicting places around the world in an exotic manner, places that we have to explore being modern, exotic signs that we have to consume. The growing middle classes have that kind of expectation, yet many do not have the resources, as was the case in 1990s China when Window of the World and Splendid China were conceived. At that time, international travel for Chinese was highly restricted, with tour groups often being the only way to travel.

Yet, as some of the data revealed, this is not the case anymore for many Chinese, and the freedom to travel to all of the places within China and around the world is easier than ever. Thus it seems to perform a niche tourism role, as will be discussed shortly, as a tourist site about tourist sites that can be enjoyed on its own.

Façadism

There is little to consume at these two parks other than signs of famous sites, and this is entirely far too easy to do. The park promoters and visitors alike praise that you can see 'all of the world' or 'all of China' in a short time, but they are, instead, consuming signs of having visited all around the world or all around China.

The miniature facades are consumed only for their aesthetic, tangible value. Details and accuracy are important and, it seems, are the only important thing as the signs are the only thing at the parks that can be consumed. The actual placement of the mini buildings in any kind of urban or suburban cultural space is entirely unimportant and unnecessary. The most detailed urban view is of New York's Lower Manhattan, yet that can only be observed from a distance.

Some attempts are also made to enhance the details by including miniature figurines of people and animals in and around the various buildings. Yet they are stationary and frozen in time; you can learn no more from the mini-monks about their religious customs and belief systems than you could from a painting. Or, at least what you can learn is the façade of their religion and habits, just as much as you can learn from the architectural design of the buildings and representations of global aesthetic forms.

The parks are inevitably interwoven with their real-life counterparts and exist entirely in opposition to them and in support of their realness.

Interestingly, some tourists do tend to say they enjoy the educational value of the miniatures and cultural performances, but this is outweighed by those who enjoy the fakery of it.

Authentic Fakery

The distance between intangible and tangible culture can be no more distant than at a miniature replica park such as this. At the same time, both of these sites are typical places where tourists go to enjoy the fakeness of the miniatures. They do it so they can tell interesting stories of all the fake miniatures they have seen to their friends and with posts on social media. They do it so they can say that they 'travelled all over the world' or 'travelled all over China' in a truly ironic sense that both the tourist and their friends can enjoy. There is no sense that people take these kind of places too seriously. It is simply an easily accessible place where people can cross libidinal boundaries safely and without too much investment of time and money. It is a good place to take photos of the fakeness and to pose with the miniatures to highlight the inauthenticity of it all.

It is also ironic, perhaps purposefully so, that a place like Shenzhen, lacking sufficient cultural heritage assets of its own to support a culture-based tourism industry like nearby Hong Kong or Guangzhou, and based on 'copying' and imitating technology coming from Hong Kong and the west, could only create tourist sites that are also based on copying.

In Window of the World, the cultural performances, such as they are, exist in the most detached and commodified way possible. They have not performed anywhere near the 'local' area and certainly not by 'natives' or 'cultural custodians' to any extent. Although this varies from year to year and was affected by the COVID-19 pandemic, we can see from reviews and interviews complaints about the maintenance of the sites' facades; tourists do not want to be reminded of the fakeness of it all so readily as the real sites.

5 Replication

This chapter will examine tourism sites that are themed after foreign places. This trend started in the colonial-era World Expositions in the nineteenth century and later formed the basis for Disney attractions such as Epcot Center's World Showcase. Las Vegas developers then started using this foreign theming in the 1960s with the construction of the Ancient Rome-themed Caesar's Palace, and later with the Egyptian-themed Luxor and Venice-themed Venetian in the 1990s. The iconic Vegas strip was the result of this development, with an assemblage of replicated world attractions like the Eiffel Tower, the mysterious black Luxor Pyramid, and various other themed hotels and casinos.

As Urry and Larson (2011, p. 129) note, malls and tourist attractions around the world "learnt lessons from Las Vegas and Disney," causing their sites to be "virtually nothing but surface effects, images, decorations and ornaments." In the end, they are simply "a glossy visual feast: an ecstasy of looking" which "quotes vicariously from historical forms" (ibid). Macau too carried on with this new tradition, developing casinos in the early twenty-first century, as their Las Vegas-based developers, such as Sands and Winn, attempted to broaden the appeal of Macau as a Las Vegas of the East. Similarly, themed tourist shopping malls, such as the Italy-themed Mediterranean Harbor at the Tokyo DisneySea, Japan, Terminal 21 in Bangkok, Thailand, West Edmonton Mall, Canada, and the Trafford Centre, Manchester, UK, show the growing interest in experiencing signs of foreign cultures without ever travelling abroad.

While Macau has several foreign-themed casinos, such as the Parisian and the Londoner, this chapter will explore the Venetian Macau due to its usage of the Italianate symbolism of Venice, an archetype of tourism aesthetics replicated in many locations around the world (see Hom 2010, 2015). The second site examined is the replica of the Austrian village of Hallstatt in Huizhou, a lesser known site, but still famous in its own right.

These sites differ in their replication strategies, from simply attempting to replicate foreign architecture and styles like in Hallstatt Huizhou, to replicating already replicated tourist sites of Las Vegas, in the case of Venetian Macau. This is also a major trend in tourism in China and around the world as localities and businesses search for attractive aesthetic themes (facades, styles, foreign

DOI: 10.4324/9781003291817-5

architecture) in order to draw tourists while ignoring the intangible culture and traditions that are integral to the cultural meaning of such buildings.

Venetian Macau

Casinos in Macau, influenced by Las Vegas, have replicated tourist attractions and aesthetic forms from Venice, Paris, London, Hollywood, and other Western cities and countries. Such sites tend to recapture an aesthetic sense of the original locations, themselves famous tourist attractions. The smelly canals of Venice are replaced by the well-chlorinated canal of the Venetian Casino in Macau. The Venetian Casino in China itself is a replica of the Venetian Casino in Las Vegas, which is itself an idealized representation of aesthetic elements from Venice, Italy.

The Venetian Macau opened in August 2007 as part of a massive property of inter-connected buildings that also features The Parisian, opened in 2016, The Plaza Macau and Four Seasons Hotel, which opened in 2008, and ancillary features, such as the multi-purpose 15,000-seat Cotai Area and the Cotai Expo centre. The whole property is owned and operated by the Macau-based Sands China Limited, a subsidiary of the Las Vegas Sands Corporation. Their five properties attracted a total of 73.7 million visitors in 2016, which is an average of 201,300 visitors per day (Sands China Limited 2016 Annual Report: 6) and earned a profit of US$1.22 billion (ibid: 4).

The Venetian is located in Cotai, a parcel of reclaimed land in Macau finished in 2005 which joined the northern island of Taipa and the southern island of Coloane. It is often termed the Cotai Strip after the Las Vegas Strip due to the development of dozens of other report properties in the area, by Sands Corporation and Wynn from Las Vegas as well as Galaxy and Melco from Hong Kong.

Sands itself was one of the original hotel casinos in Las Vegas starting in the 1950s; however, it was bought by entrepreneur Sheldon Adelson and others in the 1980s, demolished in the 1990s and replaced by the Venetian in 1999. This trend of themed casinos was nominally started with the Excalibur Casino in the 1970s and followed by New York and Paris-themed ones soon after. After their expansion to China with Venetian Macau in the early 2000s they moved on to Singapore, developing the Marina Bay Sands resort. Back in Macau, the Sands Cotai Central resort, which opened in 2012, was refurbished and rebranded as the Londoner Macau in 2021, continuing the expansion of such themed properties.

The Venetian Macao is a replica of the Venetian Les Vegas, which is a replica of Venice, Italy. The resort consists of hotel rooms, restaurants, a stadium, a casino, shopping malls, theatre halls, conference rooms, and various other indoor architects themed after Venice City, including an artificial canal with Gondola boats. The integration of those elements into a grand all-in-one resort has led to a remarkable visitation from families, business visitors, and entertainment seekers from all over the world. The whole resort is one magnificent building with 3000 hotel rooms and other venues, covering an area of 10.5 million square feet. As claimed in the 2019 annual report of Sands China Ltd., "We believe The Venetian Macao is the most visited integrated resort in Asia, and since its opening in 2007, the property has received over 366 million visitations as of December 31, 2019" (Sands China Ltd., 2020, p. 19).

The most important feature and what gives The Venetian Macao its Venice vibe is perhaps the "Grand Canal Shopping Center" (now named The Venetian Shopping Center). It is the largest indoor shopping mall in Macao, consisting of over 350 shops and various restaurants spread around three separate canals of 390 feet each – Grand Canal, St. Lucca Canal, and Marco Polo Canal. The entire Center is ceiled with a canopy of computer-animated sky with clouds, faking the indoor mall into looking like an outdoor area. Here, visitors can not only shop from brand-name vendors and dine in restaurants with cuisines from all around the world, but also pay to take Gondola rides in the canals and enjoy the Venice-like views created by the fake sky and exquisite European building walls, bridges, and decorations.

Previous Studies

Most relevant to this study is the work of Hom (2010) who examined Venice- and Italy-inspired tourist sites in Las Vegas (the Venetian Hotel and Casino) and Japan (Tokyo DisneySea). Both locations are touted to be 'cultural tourist' sites where one can experience authentic Italian culture. Yet the result is that "Italy-as-commodity becomes cloned" in that it is "simultaneously itself and yet does not resemble itself, for it has been re-inscribed as a touristic construct" (Hom 2010, p. 178). Italy is presented as a series of signs of Italy, concrete architectural forms, replicas of famous bridges, churches, and other notable buildings, and immaterial activities, like taking a ride on a gondola. Hom (2010) notes that Italy is a major source of simulacra production in tourist sites around the world. Her study focuses mainly on Italy-inspired tourist areas in Las Vegas and Japan. She argues that the prevalence of the Italian cultural aesthetic is due to Italy's "long and rich history of mass tourism" where in it has been presented as "authentic" and a place where people "live a life of leisure" (Hom 2010, p. 377).

The Venetian Macau contains some performances of Italian-style performing arts, such as acrobatic performances and singing. Even the gondoliers performed various Italian opera songs, as well as a variety of international pop songs as requested by the passengers. This is a kind of representation of Italian (and international) intangible cultural heritage, although it does not include the "involvement of communities" (du Cros and McKercher 2015, p. 83) from which the culture originates, or at least the involvement is unclear and flexible based on the staffing.

The Venetian Hotel and Casino in Las Vegas feature "a jumble of monuments," an "assemblage of buildings and facades easily identifiable as being from Venice," and "other touches" which "evoke a sense of Venice," including "striped gondola poles and shaded porticoes" (Hom 2010, p. 379). However, Hom notes that "the eye does not gravitate to one monument in particular," instead being "forced to trace a path among all of them, thus forcing "the tourist gaze to experience its re-constructed montage" (Hom 2010, p. 381, following Urry 1990b; Urry and Larson 2011). The description of Las Vegan Venetian is eerily similar to that of Venetian Macau:

> Inside, visitors stroll along the Grand Canal, shopping and dining under an artificial and air-conditioned sky that mimics sunset and sunrise according to the time of day. One encounters carabinieri and gondoliers who do not speak Italian, but who do speak English with phony Italian accents. . . . In this simulacrum, all cultural knowledge about Italy need not apply.
>
> (Hom 2010, p. 382)

Similarly, the site is filled with themed souvenirs and experiences which give Venetian and Italianate signs, yet they remain cultural products completely disassociated with cultural assets. Hom goes on to describe: "the Venetian sells all manner of physical souvenirs (i.e., carnival masks) and immaterial experiences (i.e., gondola rides) that are meant to evoke the true history of Venice while also generating profits, commodification par excellence" (Hom 2010, p. 382)

This forces us to ask the question, what is the result of cultural and heritage tourism being based not on the historical culture of the site but on signs of that culture instead? For example, the Venetian casino in Macau is a copy of the Venetian casino in Las Vegas which is a copy of Venice, a city already inundated with tourists and increasingly lacking a strong traditional Venetian culture. Tourists go to Italy's Venice to consume signs of Venice, yet the signs they consume in Las Vegas' Venetian are replicas of those signs, while the signs in Macau's Venetian are copies of copies of signs.

Aesthetic Analysis

The casino parts of the Venetian are largely indistinguishable from other casinos around the world and are thus of not much interest. The Venice part of the Venetian consists of little more than a single-floor shopping mall, circular in shape. In the middle of the mall, there is a canal of crystal-clear water, smelling of chlorine, looping around almost the entire circle. On top is a sky-blue ceiling, complete with fluffy white clouds. The canal and the sky/ceiling are far superior to the canals in Venice. The canal lacks the distinctive stench of the canals in Venice. The sky/ceiling lacks the ability to rain or shine and is always blue, even in the evenings. This gives it a casino-like sense of timelessness.

Along the sides of the canal are the shops, only taking up space on the ground floor. Above the shops are Venetian-style facades replete with fake bricks and fake windows, the latter leading not into a residence or hotel but to nothing. The

Figure 5.1 Photos from Venetian Macau

shops and restaurants themselves have little to do with Venice or Italian culture, food, or products. They are simply the same international brands one finds in airports and high-end shopping malls around the world, allowing us to safely consume in the same international cosmopolitan elite manner.

Gondolas are present as well, although their utility is largely the same as in Venice-proper. Consume the experience of being pushed around in the gondola by a distinctively dressed gondolier who will sing to you in Italian, if you pay extra. It is not for transportation either locally. This is, perhaps, the most authentic part of the experience, other than the fact the Venetian canal can only lead you back to where you began your trip.

The circular nature of the Venetian shopping mall and the endless stream of shops and restaurants is seemingly designed to trap its inhabitants. If you want to leave you have to walk for nearly the entire circumference. The exits are few and purposefully marked poorly. This gives the interested shopper little motivation to leave and the disinterested ones a feeling of being stuck in a never-ending cycle of medium-to-high-level consumer products.

Interview Analysis

The Venetian Macau (VM), due to its nature of being more of a shopping mall and entertainment centre, obviously had different motivations, with half of the respondents noting that they had only come there to do shopping, all of them have come only for a day trip from nearby cities. An additional two were only there having come to attend a concert later that day. The fame of the site was only given as a motivation by two of the foreign respondents. All in all the range of motivations for visiting was very limited, and unlike Window of the World and Splendid China, no one had noted they had come simply to take photos or "have a look."

Only three respondents replied affirmatively about the authenticity' of the Venetian Macau, mostly based on the beautiful aesthetics of the mall: "I think it's attractive. It's authentic" (VM11), "It's ok, beautiful. Authentic" (VM9). "Authenticity is ok" (VM10). "it's interesting to look at the unique design" (VM8).

Two commented directly about the fake sky overhead, one claiming "The first time the sky is very real but the more I came and looked at it the faker it is to me" (VM6), while the other noted that "My grandma didn't even know the sky is fake" (VM11).

One mentioned being disappointed at the disconnect between the images of the Venetian and the proper place: "When you look at it in the pictures you cannot tell. Only when you are here you can tell it's not real" (VM1), while another was generally disappointed: "Shall I tell the truth? It's just okay. Not very authentic. Too small" (VM5).

A Japanese-Filipino couple, who had been to Venice, Italy before, noted that "compared to real Venice its better because its much cleaner" (VM2). Meanwhile, as with other places, three responded they are unable to judge the authenticity because they have not been to the 'real' Venice. Their motivation for coming was simple because "it's just a place for fun" (VM2).

The mixed-use aspect of the Venetian Macau also plays an important role. Two came for a concert and were exploring the canal area beforehand. Four others, from across the border in either Zhuhai or Guangzhou, simply came there to do shopping.

Review Analysis

As it is more internationally oriented, reviews were found in Chinese on cTrip.com and thousands in English from TripAdvisor.

cTrip

Many reviews highlighted the Gondola ride and the foreign gondoliers, praising their ability to sing well and knowing songs in different languages, but not really commenting on the authenticity. For example, most talked about the

- "shows luxury and elegance and romance, is a good place for tourism and vacation" (Jin, 2023–03–21)
- "really romantic!" (Lv, 2022–12–21)
- "Different scenery, unique charm" (Bu, 2023–01–30)
- "although there are a lot of high-end hotels built in Macau now, but it's still a classic place" (You, 2023–01–17)
- "great view, great experience, fun and fun"

(D48, 2020–08–25)

Several related it to Venice itself, one saying "It's like being in Venice" (Kai, 2023–01–07), with another commenting "It is a miniature version of Venice in Italy" (Lv, 2022–12–21). One was more specific, highlighting specific elements that they enjoyed, saying it is "an elegant and spectacular display of Venice's 16th-century Renaissance style. . . . It fully showcases the charming scenery of the water city of Venice, Italy, with its typical arch bridges, small canals, and flagstone roads" (Zhen, 2022–10–12).

Others praised its cleanliness, "The resort environment is clean and tidy" (freel9, 2023–03–21), and its child-friendly nature, "suitable for children to play" (WeCh, 2021–08–21). Only one mentioned photography, saying it is "suitable for ladies to take pictures" (WeCh, 2021–08–21).

One comment was particularly interesting, addressing directly the inauthenticity of the Venetian. "It's kind of like the real Venice water city. A knock-off [山寨一下]." The expression 山寨 [shan zai] is usually used to describe "cheap imitation products" or "copycat wares" typically associated with Chinese-made goods, but can also refer to parodies or an ambiguous attitude one may hold towards consuming counterfeit goods (Landsberger 2019, p. 218).

TripAdvisor

Due to the much higher level of reviews for Venetian Macau, many of which specifically dealt with the hotel itself (check-in procedures, luggage, free cake, etc.), the search parameters were made more specific, using the "gondola ride," "artificial sky," and "grand canal" terms under the "popular mentions" filter. After examining 27 reviews, we reached saturation as they started to become repetitive.

The main theme related to authenticity is the relationship of the site to that of Venice itself, with reviewers using a wide variety of language to indicate this, such as 'built around,' 'based on, 'replicate,' simulate,' 'imitate,' 'mimic,' and 'resemble':

- "**built around the design** of Venice" (VM10–2017a)
- "**based on** the Venice city" (VM9–2018)
- "**attempts to replicate** the Grand Canal in Venice" (VM12–2018)
- "**replicas** of the streets in Venice" (VM12–2017)
- "**simulated** the entire ceiling in the central court area to **resemble** an evening sky and a gondola ride to **imitate** the one in Venice" (VM10–2018a)
- "unique **imitation** of Italian-Venetian architecture (VM11–2016)
- "a masterpiece in architectural **mimickery** [sic]" (VN5–2019b)

This shows clear appreciation for the effort put into the façade of the Venetian, and the different ways it is described show that tourists are not only aware of the replicated nature of the mall, but that it forms a core part of its nature and their motivation for visiting.

Others are more emotional in their comparison, talking about memories and feelings, seemingly influenced by their previous mediated encounters with Venice via the media:

- "The Canal shops and a gondola ride can transport anyone to memories of Venice" (VM10–2018b)
- "The grand canal reminds you of Venice itself" (VM11–2017)
- "created [a] Venice like feel" (VM8–2018)
- "gives you a feel[ing] as if you have been transported to Venice" (VM8–2016)
- "left no stone unturned to make you feel like you are in Venice" (VM6–2018)

One review even positively compared the Venetian Macau to the one in Las Vegas:

> Have stayed at the Venetian in Las Vegas and loved it so much that we just had to stay in the Venetian in Macao. It is just as beautiful and grand as expected. The detail in the various canals, streets and squares is unbelievable. (VM10–201b)

Interestingly, others praised the ceiling of the Grand Canal area, which is brightly lit and painted to resemble a sky.

- "false sky lightings [sic] is awesome" (VM5–2018)
- "the ceiling is painted like sky keeping it daytime 24 hours" (VM6–2018)
- "the whole experience of walking under the false sky ceiling was beautiful"

(VM8–2017)

Two were more diminutive, calling it "a mini Venice" (VM11–2018a) and "a little Venice in [China]" (VM1–2019). Only one was entirely dismissive of the attempts to replicate the Venetian aesthetic (VN5–2019b):

> I only give this a 'fair' rating because I wasn't impressed by the bling and poor imitation. Don't get me wrong, it is a fantastic spectacle, huge complex with something for almost everyone, a real eye opener. Even though it is fantastic, I felt cheap and dirty by walking through a faux St Marks Square, Grand Canal, Bridge of Sighs, gondolas etc, etc, etc. It is a masterpiece in architectural mimickery, but just a bit wrong.

Additional responses praised the photogenic quality of the site, two referencing Instagram directly:

- "Their ceilings showcased the artworks of worldclass famous artists in the romantic era worthy of your IG [Instagram] account!" (VM2–2018)
- "Everything here is beautiful to be captured and instagramable" (VM5–2019a)
- "After we wake up, you can go down to the third floor to take the picture of the artificial sky"

(VM9–2022)

Finally, a large amount of praise was given to the gondola rides, for example: "We also did the Gandola [ride] which was pitch-perfect with an Italian guy singing love songs to us" (VM8–2017) and "Kids enjoyed the Gondola ride and he sung [an] old Bollywood Hindi hit" (VM5–2018). As with the Las Vegan Venetian, the gondoliers are multicultural and multilingual due to the diversity of their clientele. Interestingly, in contemporary Italian Venice the gondoliers perform a similar role, acting as products for tourists to consume instead of a means of transportation. So the Venetian Macau gondolas are copies of the Las Vegan gondolas which are copies of the Venetian gondolas, which are commodified versions of traditional gondolas which served a functional purpose.

Hallstatt Huizhou

> Hallstatt, which was built up around the salt mining industry, first reached widespread prominence in the early 19th century when it was 'discovered' by romantic writers and artists, as struck by the beauty of Baroque architecture as the Instagrammers are today.
>
> (Street 2020)

As with the Venetian, Hallstatt Huizhou is a replica of a famous European tourist site. Austrian Hallstatt, like Italian Venice, is suffering from overtourism. On the one hand, Volodymyr Mazurok, who runs Hallstatt's Instagram account, notes that "photos of Hallstatt, compared to other cities, gather tremendous number of likes and views" (quoted in Street 2020). Yet on the other one tourist in Hallstatt, Austria, told CNN Travel that "It was honestly difficult to take certain photos without having other tourists in the background as well" and that, compared to Amsterdam and Venice, Hallstatt was "under-prepared for the level of tourists that were there, especially on a holiday weekend," and that the other tourists were only taking pictures, not being involved in any other activities (quoted in Street 2020).

Officials in Austrian Hallstatt are not oblivious to the situation: "It's equally a blessing and a curse for the locals. . . . On the one hand they have a large profit from tourism. But it comes at a cost of privacy and comfort" (Volodymyr Mazurok, quoted in Street 2020). Michelle Knoll, office manager for Hallstatt's tourism board, noted the problem of overtourism would be addressed by limiting the number of tour busses that enter the village and giving preference to overnight tourists or those who have booked other services such as visits to the museum or a cruise (Street 2020).

Most notably, the Austrian Hallstatt is becoming "particularly popular among Asian tourists, fueled in part by the fact there's a Chinese replica of the village" (Street 2020). "Fewer than 50 Chinese tourists visited Hallstatt in 2005, but now thousands fly to the Austrian town every year, according to officials from the Austrian delegation in China" (Wu 2012).

As with the Venetians in Macau and Las Vegas, a replica was built abroad, this time in a suburb of Huizhou, an industrial city, the sixth-largest in Guangdong province, finished in 2011. It is intrinsically more a commercial project than a cultural site compared to other cases in this book. Part of the complex is a real estate project of apartment complexes by the subsidiary of the Chinese state-owned real estate corporation China Minmetals Group (Bai 2014). The fact that most reports in Chinese about Hallstatt Huizhou are about the real estate project implies that the town was "moved" from Austria to Southern China to add marketing peculiarity to the real estate project than to bring cultural connotation of the authentic European elements. According to the manager of the real estate development company, the town has recorded hundreds of thousands of visitors since its opening (Bai 2014).

Still, Hallstatt Huizhou needed some validation from the original source. Luckily, on June 2, 2012, the mayor of Hallstatt, Austria, visited Hallstatt Huizhou to attend the opening ceremony and sign a cultural exchange agreement (Spiegel Reise 2012). "While parts of the Hallstatt population viewed the Chinese plans with scepticism, mayor Alexander Scheutz said that he saw a chance in the project for the tourism in the 'original' Hallstatt" (Spiegel Reise 2012). The consequence is that "local authorities in Hallstatt have since softened their stance, seeing a rare, marketing opportunity at the heart of one of the world's fastest growing tourism markets" (Wu 2012).

Aesthetic Analysis

On close inspection, it is very clear this is a shallow replica of Austrian culture – a town of facades, with no underlying Austrian intangible cultural elements. Food is for Chinese tourists, fried noodles and rice and ice cream. The closest is a Western-looking restaurant which is actually a franchise of the 'Gong Cha' national brand of tea shops, adorned with random English words stuck on the wall, fake flowers, and instant coffee and oily Chicken schnitzel as the only 'western' offerings.

Around the site are signs in German, ostensibly for restaurants, titled 'Meeresfrüchte Speiselokal,' seafood dinner, but with printouts of unrelated menus from a Texas Chinese restaurant and Florida pizza place attached below. Or a wooden fish with the words 'Feinschmecker Treffpunkt" or a gourmet meeting place.

The most recognizable landmark is the church, of course not used as a church. The outside is composed of stone-like tiles glued onto concrete. The original is a stone church, but no effort was made even to construct the church in a similar manner. The church in Hallstatt Huizhou is similar to one described by du Cros and McKercher, in that "the interior is devoid of any reference to Christianity" and weddings held there would be "completely lacking any of the associated intangible cultural significance and meaning associated with Christian weddings" (du Cros and McKercher 2015, p. 95).

The description in the 'Scenic Introduction' sign near the entrance notes the specific land area of the site, going on to claim "The Austrian architectural style and European-style culture are perfectly blended in this unique mountain and water heritage, and come out with a variety of exotic buildings and facilities," listing a "cultural square, music square, beer square, commercial pedestrian street" amongst others. Its last claim is that the site has the "perfect integration of the authentic Austrian European exoticness, Chinese traditional culture and Lingnan culture."

Figure 5.2 Photos from Hallstatt Huizhou

Review Analysis

The site could not be found listed on TripAdvisor or other international tourism apps, so this analysis will rely only on cTrip reviews. Also, due to the travel restrictions during the pandemic, there is a gap of around 2 years in the reviews, with few being posted from 2020 to 2022. It appears that reviews of Hallstatt Huizhou mention authenticity/similarities more than other sites. On the other hand, most reviews were negative and focused on complaining about the price, stating that the views are not worth 50 RMB because the site is too small and simple, and the selection of shops was small.

Reviews mentioning authenticity, like with the Venetian, used terms such as 'imitation,' Austrian/European-style or flavour, and 'modeled after' to compare this site to the original. One review, who had apparently been to Hallstatt in Austria, praised the site, saying "I feel that Minmetals has made great efforts to **imitate** the town" (M32, 2023–03–24). Another disagreed, saying "The town is very different from the real town of Hallstatt" (YX1, 2023–03–04), although it was not clear from the review if they had been there or not. The remainder talk about 'imitation,' 'flavour,' and 'style,' all indicating appreciation of the façade they consumed:

- "designed to **imitate** a European town, giving a feeling that you are in a foreign country" (Fei, 2019–10–26)
- "The two sides are full of **Austrian-style buildings**. . . . This scene is indeed very **European-style** Chinese architecture (Shuang, 2019–06–21)
- "The whole place is **modeled after** the **European-style**, with parts of the building even copied" (Khcc, 2019–11–24)
- "the central square has a bit of a **European flavor**" (YX1, 2023–03–04)

"the architecture is exotic" (Bai, 2023–02–08)

One (M46, 2023–02–13) mentioned the only reason they went was because it has "the name of some European town" but then advised that it is better to visit Shamian in Guanzhou, the former colonial district with European-style buildings, or the Kaiping Diaolou, referencing the World Heritage site containing dozens of watchtower-style buildings build by overseas Chinese over 100 years ago and inspired by Western architecture.

Four explicitly mentioned the site being photogenic, that it's "good to take wedding photos" (Wang 2019–9–9) and "used as a backdrop for wedding photos" (Khcc, 2019–11–24), or more generally that it is "more suitable for taking photos" (Fei, 2019–10–26) and is "the best place for friends who like to take photos" (Bai, 2023–02–08).

Finally, one claimed visiting the site inspired them: "I'd like to visit a real [真正] Austrian town sometime" (Wang 2019–9–9).

Conclusion

Effect of Media

While both Venice and Hallstatt are famous due to contemporary media, they are largely incomparable as Venice and Italy are the founding elements of tourism and act as core signs of tourism. Venice itself acts as a universal floating signifier of tourism which predates modern tourism yet permeates our very concept of modern tourism.

Austrian Hallstatt is more of a regional Europe-famous site, by contrast, yet as noted earlier, it is suffering from overtourism similar to how it is affecting Venice. Its status as the rumoured inspiration for the town of Arendelle in Disney's *Frozen* franchise does not help alleviate this. It rose to be a European tourist destination due to its own characteristics as a beautiful village on a scenic lake in the Alps that nearby urbanites can escape to. This, combined with the decline of its mining industry, led to its growing dependence on tourism. It is highly picturesque nature lends itself to photography and, currently, social media such as Instagram.

Yet Hallstatt Huizhou does not carry the same baggage as the Austrian version. It is not acclaimed by the Chinese due to being a replica of the specific Austrian Hallstatt but in a more general way as a European-looking place to take pictures, consume signs of Europe, and relax. But the same can also be said for Venetian Macau, as the idea of 'Venice' has become so abstract people do not go to consume a specific replica of Italian Venice but of Venetian simulacra.

Hallstatt Huizhou is a top-down inspiration in that there was no local demand for a place that replicated an unknown Austrian village. It comes from the travels of the Minimetal Company CEO who himself thought it would be a good place to replicate because he enjoyed it so much.

Façadism

Sites like the Macanese Venetian are themed in that they draw their aesthetic sense from a limited collection of signs of Italian Venice in order to attract tourists to the signs of Venetian Venice. No tourist going there would ever think it is the same thing as Italian Venice; they are better than Venetian Venice. The canals do not smell, you do not have to worry about interfering with the local population as there is no local population, you have a wide selection of international brands and cuisines, you can stay in a hotel very close by, touristically speaking Macanese and Las Vegan Venetians are more convenient than Italian Venice and the lack of 'authentic' Venice matters little. The spectacle of being in a replica of Venice, one that is designed to have its signs of Venice reproduced through holiday photos, and now social media, is the purpose.

If a tourist went to Italian Venice they would still only be able to consume the signs of Venice, not 'authentic' Venice, and Italian Venice's signs might not meet the high standards set by mediated representations and stereotypes of Venice. For example, as discussed in the review analysis, the appreciation of the gondola rides shows how many levels deep the simulation is; the move from actually useful transportation in Venice to a tourist attraction in Venice to a replicated experience in Las Vegas to a copy of that experience in Macau. The point is to consume the signs of a gondola ride and the gondolier singing so that you can say you have done it, along with some snapshots of you with the gondolier in their white and red-striped shirt.

Authentic Fakery

Again, as the counterpart of façadism, the fakeness of both of these sites becomes the motivation for visiting the site. It is a feature, not a bug. As Boorstin says, "We go not to test the image by the reality, but to test reality by the image" (Boorstin 1961, p. 116).

For the Venetian, the authentic fakery is performed at two levels. First is to enjoy the fakery of the Venetian Macau in contrast to the Italy Venetian. Second is to enjoy the fakery of the Venetian Macau in contrast to the Las Vegan Venetian in contrast to the Italian Venetian. In fact, enjoying the fakery is the primary motivation for travelling to both of these sites.

6 Conclusion

Media Influence

This study explored the intriguing relationship between historical sites, tourism, and the influence of media in shaping our anticipation, decoding, and re-encoding of tourist sites. It highlighted how the popularity of historical dramas and the dissemination of historical knowledge through education have become strong motivations for travellers to visit historical sites in China and other countries. The ability to capture and share photos on social media has further amplified this trend.

We also shed light on the phenomenon of dressing up in period costumes and the proliferation of historical clothing rental shops at these sites. Such practices have become important rituals for young tourists, driven by the influence of media and cultural exchanges between countries. The desire to relive elements of the past, albeit superficially, indicates a yearning for nostalgia and a temporary escape from the fast-paced modern world.

Moreover, the text emphasized the appeal of these preserved and reconstructed sites as refuges for urban dwellers seeking respite from the hustle and bustle of city life. By idealizing the purity and simplicity of the past, these sites offer a sense of tranquillity and a connection to nature. Their proximity to urban areas and the inclusion of parks and natural surroundings further contribute to their allure.

The ubiquity of world-famous attractions, both in real life and through various forms of media, ensures that there is something for everyone at these sites. Regardless of one's level of education or travel experience, these attractions serve as recognizable symbols that draw people in. We highlighted how the fame associated with these attractions becomes a self-referential motivation for visitors, reinforcing their desire to experience and capture these iconic landmarks.

In examining the cases of Venice, Hallstatt, and the replication of European aesthetics in Huizhou, the text revealed the complex interplay between media, tourism, and cultural consumption. These places have become not just destinations in themselves but also symbols that represent broader cultural

DOI: 10.4324/9781003291817-6

aspirations and desires. They are ideal sites of pseudo-authenticity as their allure and photogenic qualities have made them highly sought-after locations for photography and social media sharing.

Ultimately, this exploration prompts us to question our relationship with the past and our consumption of history. These sites are not simply remnants of a bygone era, but rather products of modernization, globalization, and the media-driven world we inhabit. They reflect our fascination with the exotic, our yearning for connection, and our desire to escape the confines of our everyday lives.

Authentic Fakery

There are many unique characteristics and motivations behind visiting sites that embody fakeness and pseudo-authenticity. It has explored the case of Huitong Village, highlighting that while it is a preserved ancient village, its appeal lies more in its façades and sanitized signs of ancient villages rather than its fakery. On the other hand, Mt. Yunji, as a reconstructed site, captivates visitors with its untarnished, pseudo-authentic experience, detached from the realities of actual organic development. These sites represent the extreme distance between intangible and tangible culture, where miniature replica parks like these exist.

Interestingly, both Window of the World and Splendid China serve as places where tourists can revel in the fakeness of the facades. It becomes a source of amusement and storytelling for visitors to share their experiences of encountering these fake miniatures with friends and on social media. There is an ironic sense of having "traveled all over the world" or "traveled all over China" in experiencing these sites, highlighting the playful nature of the visit. The fakeness of these places is not taken too seriously; rather, they offer an easily accessible and safe space for crossing libidinal boundaries without significant time or financial investment. Visitors can capture photos of the inauthenticity and pose with the miniatures, accentuating the artificiality of it all.

Ironically, Shenzhen, lacking substantial cultural heritage assets of its own, has resorted to creating tourist sites based on copying and imitating. Window of the World exemplifies this by offering cultural performances in a detached and commodified manner, often performed far from the local area and by individuals who are not necessarily native or cultural custodians. Reviews and interviews reveal tourists' preference for maintaining the illusion of authenticity, as they do not want to be constantly reminded of the fakeness inherent in these sites, unlike real historical sites.

Furthermore, the fakeness itself becomes a significant motivation for visiting these sites, as highlighted by Boorstin's notion that people do not visit to test the image against reality, but rather to test reality against the image. The Venetian in Macau exemplifies this authentic fakery on two levels: first, in enjoying the contrast between the Venetian Macau and the Venetian in Italy, and second, in appreciating the contrast between the Venetian Macau, the Venetian in Las Vegas, and the Venetian in Italy. The enjoyment of fakery becomes the primary incentive for travelling to these sites.

In essence, this exploration of fakeness and pseudo-authenticity in tourism sheds light on the intricate dynamics between cultural consumption, media influence, and the desire for unique experiences. These sites represent a form of escapism, where visitors can temporarily immerse themselves in artificial worlds and create narratives around their encounters. While they may lack the depth and historical authenticity of genuine heritage sites, these fakes provide a space for playfulness, exploration, and the suspension of reality.

Façadism

Mt Yunji stands out due to its complete reliance on facades, devoid of any local presence or original intangible culture. It offers visitors the imagery of old buildings in an idyllic hillside setting, detached from historical context and reconstituted within a theme park. On the other hand, Huitong Village represents a more typical model of cultural preservation, where increased infrastructure and beautification efforts have transformed the village into a tourist destination. However, the departure of locals has led to the filling of village facades with restaurants, cafes, and other amenities necessary for tourists.

Huitong Village relies heavily on its historical significance as a strong village during the turn of the century and the warlord period in Guangzhou. The preservation of two diaolou and an ancestral hall, although not as impressive as other examples, serves as justification for its conservation. Both sites present sanitized depictions of classical China, surpassing existing classical villages in standards of beautification and aesthetic appeal. While countless similar villages across China possess living cultural assets, they remain underdeveloped for tourism due to the presence of locals and a lack of systematic beautification efforts. Consequently, places like Huitong are chosen as representatives of classical villages for tourists to consume, offering mere facades of an antique era devoid of authentic cultural essence.

For Window of the World and Splendid China, there is little to consume beyond signs of famous sites, which is remarkably easy to do. Visitors and promoters alike praise the opportunity to witness "all of the world" or "all of China" in a short time, but in reality, they are merely consuming signs that indicate having visited various locations. The miniature facades hold value solely for their aesthetic and tangible appeal, with details and accuracy being of utmost importance. The placement of mini buildings within an urban or suburban cultural space becomes insignificant and unnecessary. While attempts are made to enhance the details with miniature figurines, they remain static and offer limited insight into religious customs or beliefs. The parks exist in direct opposition to their real-life counterparts, supporting and showcasing their authenticity.

Some tourists claim to appreciate the educational value of the miniatures and cultural performances, but the majority are drawn to the fakery and inauthenticity of these sites. They embrace the spectacle of replicas, designed to reproduce the signs and imagery of renowned destinations, such as the Macanese Venetian. Visitors recognize that these replicas are not equivalent to their authentic counterparts, yet they offer advantages such as clean canals, the absence of interference from the local population, a variety of international brands and cuisines, and convenient accommodations. The purpose is to consume the signs of a replicated experience and capture holiday photos, later shared on social media.

Even if tourists were to visit authentic Venice, they would still consume the signs of Venice rather than the "authentic" experience. The mediated representations and stereotypes of Venice often set high standards that might not align with the reality of the place. For instance, the appreciation of gondola rides demonstrates the depth of simulation, from useful transportation in Venice to a tourist attraction to a replicated experience in Las Vegas, and finally to a copy of that experience in Macau. The focus lies in consuming the signs of a gondola ride and the presence of a gondolier, enabling visitors to boast about the experience and capture snapshots with the gondolier in their traditional attire.

Implications

We do not argue that this phenomenon is necessarily generalizable to all tourist sites, although it is likely all tourist sites contain some elements of this. We do argue that other re-constructed and preserved cultural heritage sites, miniature theme parks, and replicas of famous tourist sites can be described in a similar way. Furthermore, the context of these sites being in China is only marginally relevant as these types of tourist sites exist all over the world. These six sites are chosen due to the proximity to the author's home institution, our previous experience travelling to them, and that these specific sites are under-researched.

Future research should move out of the sphere of Antirealism and other relativistic epistemological modes. Perceptions and feelings of authenticity in tourism come from our relationship with the signs that we consume there, signs that come from models generated by our consumption of famous places, mostly from the media. We come to our tourist journeys with preconceptions in mind and judge the tourist sites not on their own merit but from our stereotypes.

The separation of tangible and intangible culture from its 'raw' form as cultural assets does not necessitate us re-constructing the authenticity that has gone missing. The signs of authenticity are all around us, and they are all we need. Tourists are perfectly fine with consuming these signs and enjoying the fakery of the experience. We are happy to consume the façades lacking any intangible cultural background as long as they meet our expectations of what the facades should look like, as long as it gives us a feeling that we have crossed some boundary and are getting a fresh look at the world. We revel in re-encoding these signs through photographs and sharing them, showing off our modernity and also our understanding that this is the best we can get.

The past is gone, traditional culture is forever changed by capitalism, and we can never travel to exotic and unknown foreign countries like our ancestors did. No matter how much research we do about authenticity, no matter how many sites we visit and the tourists and locals we interview, we have to acknowledge the current state of tourism. We travel to show our modernity, to test the preconceptions we have, and try to enjoy the fakeness as much as we can.

We can never recapture our fantasies of travel, we can only be tourists living in a world of pseudo-authenticity.

Bibliography

Arlt, W.G. and Hu, H., 2009. Tourism development and cultural interpretation in Ganzi, China. *In*: C. Ryan and H. Gu, eds. *Tourism in China: Destination, cultures and communities*. London: Routledge, 168–181.

Bai, Y., July 2014. The site selection "sequelae" of the clone Austrian Town built by Minmetals: Few people have occupied the first phase of the building for two years' [Wukuang jianshe kelongban aaodili xiaozhen xuanzhi "houyizheng": Yiqi jiaolong jin liangnian ruzhuzhe liaoliao], *nbd.com.cn*. Available from: www.nbd.com.cn/articles/2014-07-23/850758.html.

Barthes, R., 1957 [1993]. Myth today. *In*: A. Lavers, ed. and tr. *Mythologies*. New York: Vintage.

Baudrillard, J., 1970 [1990]. Mass media culture. *In*: P. Foss and J. Pefanis, trs and eds., *Revenge of the crystal*. London: Pluto.

Baudrillard, J., 1996. *The system of objects*, J. Benedict, tr. London: Verso.

Baudrillard, J., 1976 [1993]. Order of simulacra. *In*: I.H. Grant, tr., *Symbolic exchange and death*. London: Sage.

Baudrillard, J. 1970b [1990]. Mass media culture. *In:* P. Foss and J. Pefanis (trs & eds), *Revenge of the Crystal*. London: Pluto.

Baudrillard, J. 1975 [2001]. Mass (sociology of). *In:* G. Genosko (ed), B. Freedman (tr), *The Uncollected Baudrillard*. London: Sage.

Baudrillard, J. 1978b [1985]. *In:* P. Foss, J. Johnston, and P. Patton (trs), *The Shadow of the Silent Majorities*. New York: Semotext(e)

Baudrillard, J. 2000. *The Vital Illusion*. New York: Columbia University Press.

Baudrillard, J., 1978 [1994]. Precession of simulacra. *In*: P. Foss and P. Patton, trs., *Simulations*. New York: Semiotext(e)).

Baudrillard, J., 1989. *America*. London: Verso.

Baudrillard, J., 1992 [2009]. The vanishing point of communication. *In*: D.B. Clarke et al. eds., *Jean Baudrillard: Fatal theories*. London: Routledge.

Baudrillard, J., 1993. *The transparency of evil: Essays on extreme phenomena*. London: Verso.

Baudrillard, J., 1994. *Simulacra and simulations*, P. Foss, P. Patton and P. Beitchman, trs., Ann Arbor, MI: University of Michigan Press.

Belhassen, Y. and Caton, K., 2006. Authenticity matters. *Annals of Tourism Research*, 33 (3), 853–856.

Bendix, R., 1997. *Search for authenticity: The formation of folklore studies*. Madison, WI: University of Wisconsin.

Benjamin, W., 1936 [2008]. The work of art in the age of mechanical reproduction. *In*: J.A. Underwood, tr., *The work of art in the age of mechanical reproduction: Great ideas*. London: Penguin.

Boorstin, D., 1961. *The image*. New York: Vintage.

Bourdieu, P., 1984. *Distinction: A critique of the judgement of taste*. London: Routledge.

Brooks, G., 1993. Visitation to major heritage sites – Some essential planning considerations. *In*: ICOMOS, ed., *Archaeological heritage management: Cultural tourism and conservation economics. Proceedings of the ICOMOS 10th general assembly*. Colombo: ICOMOS.

Bruner, E., 1984. Text, play and story: The construction and reconstruction of self and society. *In*: *1983 Proceedings of the American ethnographic society*. Washington, DC: American Anthropological Association.

Bruner, E., 1989. Of cannibals, tourists, and ethnographers. *Cultural Anthropology*, 4 (4), 438–445.

Bruner, E., 1994. Abraham Lincoln as authentic reproduction: A critique of postmodernism. *American Anthropologist*, 96, 397–415.

Campbell, C., 1987. *The romantic ethic and the spirit of modern consumerism*. Oxford: Basil Blackwell.

Chao, X. and Wang, Q., 2021. A study on the relationship between perception of authenticity, place attachment and tourist loyalty [Zhenshixing ganzhi, defang yilian yu youke zhongcheng de guanxi yanjiu – yi Tianjin "wudadao" weili]. *Business Economic*, 2021–5, 110–20.

Chen, C. and Chen, Z., 2021. A study on the tourism commercialization symbol perception and experiential authenticity of tourists: A case study of Xi'an Huimin Street [Lvyou zhe shangyehua fuhao ganzhi yu tiyan zhenshixing yanjiu – yi Xi'an huiminjie weili]. *Journal of Zhejiang University (Science Edition)*, 48 (2), 249–260.

Chen, C. and Zhao, Z., 2021. A research of authenticity experience model of rural tourists [Xiangcun youke zhenshixing tiyan moxing yanjiu]. *Scientia Geographica Sinica*, 41 (7), 1237–1245.

Chen, L., 2014. Cultural impact of modernization and tourism on Dai villages in Xishuangbanna, China. *Tourism Geographies*, 16 (5), 757–771.

Chen, M., Yu, Z., Chen, X., Zhang, Z. and Guo, S., 2022. A comparative study on the authenticity perception of homestay between rural tourists and residents – A case study of Mingyue Village, Chengdu [Xiangcun youke yu jumin minus zhenshixing ganzhi bijiao yanjiu – Yi Chengdu Mingyuecun weili]. *Technology and Market*, 130–133.

Chen, R. and Zhou, Z., 2018. Influence of authenticity perception of culture tourism on tourists' loyalty: The mediating effects of tourists' well-being' [Wenhua lvyou zhenshixing ganzhi dui lvyouzhe zhongcheng de yingxiang jizhi yanjiu]. *Journal of Business Economics*, 1, 61–74.

Chen, W. and Su, Q., 2012. A comparative study of authenticity in tourism home and aboard [abroad] over the past fifteen years [Jin shiwunian lai zhenshixing zai guoneiwai lvyou Zhong de yanjiu duibi]. *Human Geography*, 27 (3), 118–24.

Chhabra, D., Healy, R. and Sills, E., 2003. Staged authenticity and heritage tourism. *Annals of Tourism Research*, 30 (3), 702–719.

Cohen, E., 1972. Toward a sociology of international tourism. *Social Research*, 39, 164–182.

Cohen, E., 1979a. A phenomenology of tourist experiences. *Sociology*, 13, 179–201.

Cohen, E., 1979b. Rethinking the sociology of tourism. *Annals of Tourism Research*, 6 (1), 18–35.

Cohen, E., 1988. Authenticity and commoditization in tourism. *Annals of Tourism Research*, 15, 371–385.

Cohen, E., 1995. Contemporary tourism – Trends and challenges: Sustainable authenticity or contrived post-modernity? *In*: R. Butler and D. Pearce, eds., *Change in tourism: People, places, processes*. London: Routledge, 12–29.

Cohen E. and Cohen, S., 2012. Current sociological theories and issues in tourism. *Annals of Tourism Research*, 15 (3), 2177–2202.

Cohen-Aharoni, Y., 2017. Guiding the 'real' temple: The construction of authenticity in heritage sites in a state of absence and distance. *Annals of Tourism Research*, 63, 73–82.

Cornet, J., 1975. African art and authenticity. *African Art*, 9 (1), 52–55.

Craik, J., 1997. The culture of tourism sites. *In*: C. Rojek and J. Urry, eds., *Touring cultures: Transformations of travel and theory*. London: Routledge, 113–136.

Crang, M., 2004. Cultural geographies of tourism. *In*: A.A. Lew, M. Hall and A.M. Williams, eds. *A companion to tourism*. London: Blackwell.

Culler, J., 1981. Semiotics of tourism. *American Journal of Semiotics*, 1, 127–40.

Davis, R.C. and Marvin G.R., 2004. *Venice, the tourists maze: A cultural critique of the world's most touristed city*. Berkeley: University of California Press.

Dong, X., Gao, Y. and Ma, J., 2017. A literature review and prospect of domestic tourism[:] Authenticity research in last two decades [Jin ershinian guonei lvyou "zhenshixing" yanjiu pingshu yu zhanwang]. *Journal of Chongqing Technology and Business University (Social Sciences Edition)*, 34 (5), 64–73.

Du, S. & R. Zha., 2021. Perception of Authenticity and Post-tour Behavioral Intention from the Perspective of Local Dependence – A Case Study of Hakka Wai House. *Journal of Jiaying University (Philosophy & Social Sciences)*, 39 (1), 24–28.

du Cros, H. and McKercher, B., 2020. *Cultural tourism*. 3rd ed. London: Routledge.

du Cros, H. and McKercher, B., 2015. *Cultural tourism*. 2nd ed. London: Routledge.

Eco, U., 1986. *Travels in hyperreality*. New York: Harcourt Brace & Co.

Errington, F. and Gewertz, D., 1989. Tourism and anthropology in a post-modern world. *Oceania*, 60, 37–54.

Foucault, M., 1980. *Power/knowledge: Selected interviews and other writings 1972–1977*, C. Gordon, ed., New York: Pantheon.

Franci, G., 2005. *Dreaming of Italy: Las Vegas and the virtual grand tour*. Reno and Las Vegas, NV: University of Nevada.

Gao, Y. and Zheng, Y., 2010. A comparative study on the authentic perception of landscapes in Fenghuang Ancient City' [Fenghuang gucheng jingguan zhenshixing ganzhi duibi yanjiu – jiyu minju he lvyouzhe shijiao], *Tourism Tribune*, 12, 44–52.

Goffman, E., 1959. *The presentation of self in everyday life*. Garden City, NY: Doubleday.

Graburn, N.H.H., 1983. The anthropology of tourism. *Annals of Tourism Research*, 10 (1), 9–33.

Graburn, N.H.H., 2001. Secular ritual: A general theory of tourism. *In*: V.L. Smith and M. Brent, eds. *Hosts & guests revisited: Tourism issues of the 21st century*. New York: Cognizant.

Greenwood, D.J., 1977. Culture by the pound: An anthropological perspective on tourism as cultural commoditization. *In*: V.L. Smith, ed., *Hosts and guests*. Philadelphia, PA: University of Pennsylvania Press.

Guang, X., 2012. The birth of a fake Austrian town – A look at the 'copying model' of tourism real estate [Yige shanzhaiban "Aodili xiaozhen" de dansheng – Shenshi lvyou dichan de "fuzhi moshi"]. *China Construction*, 2012, 20–22.

Guo, X., 2022. Research on contradiction and conflict behind rural tourism environmental protection and its resolution mechanism [Xiangcun lvyou huanjing baohu beihou de maodun chongtu jiqi huajie jizhi yanjiu]. *Agriculture Technology and Information*, 19, 17–20.

Haldrup, M. and Larsen, J., 2010. *Tourist, performance, and the everyday: Consuming the orient*. London: Routledge.

Hearns-Branaman, J.O., 2008. "Must we ourselves not become gods?": A perspective on the theories of Foucault, Debord and Baudrillard in explaining contemporary power structures. *International Journal of Baudrillard Studies*, 5 (2).

Hearns-Branaman, J.O., 2011. *The fourth estate in the USA and UK: Discourses of truth and power*. Thesis (PhD). Institute of Communication Studies, University of Leeds. Available from: eTheses.WhiteRose.ac.uk/2283

Hearns-Branaman, J.O., 2012. The Egyptian revolution did not take place: On the live TV coverage by Al Jazeera English. *International Journal of Baudrillard Studies*, 9 (1).

Hearns-Branaman, J.O., 2015. Towards a Hyperrealist epistemology of the news media: Baudrillard, Boorstin, Tuchman, and Hall. *International Journal of Baudrillard Studies*, 12 (2).

Hearns-Branaman, J.O., 2016. *Journalism and the philosophy of truth: Beyond objectivity and balance*. London: Routledge.

Hetherington, S., 2012. Epistemology's past here and now. *In*: S. Hetherington, ed., *Epistemology: The key thinkers*. London: Continuum.

Hobsbawm, E., 1992. Introduction: Inventing traditions. In E. Hobsbawm and T. Ranger, eds. *The invention of tradition*. Cambridge: Cambridge University.

Hobsbawm, E. and Ranger, T., 1983. *The invention of tradition*. Cambridge: Cambridge University Press.

Hom, S.M., 2010. Italy without borders: Simulacra, tourism, suburbia, and the new Grand Tour. *Italian Studies*, 65 (3), 376–397.

Hom, S.M., 2015. *The beautiful country: Tourism and the impossible state of destination Italy*. Toronto: University of Toronto Press.

Hou, L., 2022. Research on the coordinated development of rural tourism culture industry and intangible cultural heritage protection – Based on the background of comprehensive rural revitalization [Xiangcun lvyou wenhua chanye yu feiwuzhi wenhua yichan baohu xietiao fazhan yanjiu: Jiyu xiangcun quanmian zhenxing Beijing]. *Southern Journal*, 10, 27–29.

International Council on Monuments and Sites (ICOMOS), 2008. *The ICOMOS charter for the interpretation and presentation of cultural heritage sites*. Available from: www.icomos.org/images/DOCUMENTS/Charters/interpretation_e.pdf

Jin, H., Sun, G., Zhang, X. and Feng, Q., 2022. Effect of tourism authenticity on tourist's environmentally responsible behavior of traditional village: Roles of nostalgia and Taoist ecological value [Chuantong cunluo lvyou zhenshixing dui lvyouzhe huanjing zeren xingwei de yingxiang yanjiu – Huaijiu he daojia shengdai jiazhiguan de zuoyong]. *Journal of Zhejiang University (Science Edition)*, 49 (1), 121–130.

Kirshenblatt-Gimblett, B., 2004. Intangible heritage as metacultural production. *Museum International*, 56 (1/2), 52–65.

Klingmann, A., 2007. *Brandscapes*. Cambridge, MA: MIT.

Kotler, P. and Turner, R.E., 1989. *Marketing Management.* Scarborough: Prentice Hall.

Kracauer, S., 1927 [1995], *The mass ornament: Weimar essays*. Cambridge: Harvard University Press.

Lash, S., 1990. *Sociology of postmodernism*. London: Routledge.

Lash, S. and Urry, J., 1994. *Economies of signs and space*. London: Sage.

Lau, R.W.K., 2004. Critical realism and news production. *Media, Culture and Society*, 26 (5), 693–711.

Lau, R.W.K., 2010. Revisiting authenticity: A social realist approach. *Annals of Tourism Research*, 37 (2), 478–489.

Landsberger, S., 2019. Shanzhai = creativity, creativity = Shanzhai. *In*: J. de Kloet, Y.F. Chow and L. Sheen, eds., *Boredom, Shanzhai, and digitisation in the time of creative China*. Amsterdam: University of Amsterdam Press.

Li, F.M.S. and Sofield, T.H.B., 2009. Huangshan (Yellow Mountain), China: The meaning of harmonious relationships. *In*: C. Ryan and G. Huimin, eds. *Tourism in China: Destination, cultures and communities*. London: Routledge, 157–167.

Li, M., Wu, B. and Cai, L., 2008. Tourism development of world heritage sites in China: A geographic perspective. *Tourism Management*, 29 (2), 308–319.

Lin, L., Ling, S. and Chen, Z., 2016. Analysis of the density of tourists and the degree of tourism dependence in the main coastal cities in China. *Journal of Jiangnan University (Humanities & Social Sciences Edition)*, 5, 81–89.

Liu, S. and Lin, Y., 2020. Tourist participation, authenticity perception and tourism value development of Intangible Cultural Heritage [Youke canyu, zhenshixing ganzhi yu feiyiwenhua lvyou jiazhi kaifa]. *Fujian Forum – Humanities and Social Sciences Edition*, 12, 99–108.

Local Chronicle Office of Guangdong Provincial People's Government, April 2019. Xiangzhou District Tangjiawan Town Huitong Village [Xiangzhou Qu Tangjiawan Zhen Huitong Cun]. *dfz.gd.gov.cn*. Available from: http://dfz.gd.gov.cn/nycq/dcxc/content/post_2275443.html.

Longino, H.E., 2002. *The fate of knowledge*. Princeton: Princeton University.

Ma, D., 2020. The relationship between cultural authenticity, place attachment and tourism support: An empirical study from the perspective of residents in ethnic tourism villages [Wenhua yuanzhenxing, defang yilian yu lvyou zhichidu de guanxi – Jiyu minzu lvyou cunzhai jumin shijiao de shizheng yanjiu]. *Social Scientist*, 7, 51–56.

MacCannell, D., 1973. Staged authenticity: Arrangement of social space in tourist settings. *American Journal of Sociology*, 79 (3), 589–603.

MacCannell, D., 1976. *The visitor: A new theory of the leisure class*. New York: Schoken Books.

MacCannell, D., 1992. *Empty meeting grounds: The tourist papers*. London: Routledge.

MacCannell, D., 1999. *The tourist: A new theory of the leisure class*. Berkeley: University of California.

Massey, D., 1994. *Space, place and gender*. Cambridge: Polity.

McCartney, G. and Chen, Y., 2019. Co-creation tourism in an ancient Chinese town. *Journal of China Tourism Research*. https://doi.org/10.1080/19388160.2019.1596856

McKercher, B. and du Cros, H., 2002. *Cultural tourism*. London: Routledge.

McKercher, B. and du Cros, H., 2005. Cultural heritage and visiting attractions. *In*: D. Buhalis and C. Costa, eds., *Tourism business frontiers: Consumers, products and industry*. Butterworth-Heinemann, 211–219.

McLeod, M.D., 1976. Limitations of the genuine. *African Art*, 9 (3), 48–51.

McLuhan, M., 1964 [1994]. *Understanding media: The extensions of man*. Boston: MIT Press.

Meethan, K., 2004. Transnational corporations, globalization, and tourism. *In*: A.A. Lew, M. Hall and A.M. Williams, eds., *A companion to tourism*. London: Blackwell.

Meng, S., 2022. A study on the coordinated development of world cultural heritage protection and tourism in Gansu Province [Gansu shijie wenhua yichan baohu yu lvyou xietong fazhan yanjiu]. *Cooperative Economy and Technology*, 11x, 14–7.

Mirchandani, R., 2005. Postmodernism and sociology: From the epistemological to the empirical. *Sociological Theory*, 23 (1), 86–115.

Montgomery, B.M. and Baxter, L., 1998. A guide to dialectical approaches to studying personal relationships. *In*: B.M. Montgomery and L. Baxter, eds., *Dialectical approaches to studying personal relationships*. Hoboken: Lawrence Erlbaum.

Munt, I., 1994. The "other" postmodern tourism: Culture, travel and the new middle class. *Theory, Culture & Society*, 11, 101–123.

Noy, C., 2004. This trip really changed me: Backpackers' narratives of self-change. *Annals of Tourism Research*, 31 (1), 78–102.

Nuryanti, W., 1996. Heritage and postmodern tourism. *Annals of Tourism Research*, 23 (2).

Oakes, T., 1998. *Tourism and modernity in China*. London: Routledge.

OCT., n.d., About overseas Chinese town holdings company. *Chinaoct.com*. Available from: www.chinaoct.com/hqc_en/about-us.html

Olsen, K., 2002. Authenticity as a concept in tourism research: The social organization of the experience of authenticity. *Tourist Studies*, 2 (2), 159–182.

Osborne, P., 2000. Travelling light: Photography. *In*: *Travel and Visual Culture*. Manchester: Manchester University.

Park, E., Choi, B.K. and Lee, T.J., 2019. The role and dimensions of authenticity in heritage tourism. *Tourism Management*, 75, 99–109.

Pearson, M. and Sullivan, S., 1995. *Looking after heritage places: The basics of heritage planning for managers, landowners and administrators*. Melbourne: Melbourne University Press.

Pocock, D., 1992. Catherine Cookson County: Visitor expectation and experience. *Journal of Geographical Association*, 77 (3), 236–243.

Poerksen, B., 2008. The ideal and the myth of objectivity: Provocations of Constructivist journalism research. *Journalism Studies*, 9 (2), 295–304.

Rapoport, A., 1982. *The meaning of the built environment*. London: Chapman and Hall.

Rickly-Boyd, J.M., 2012. Authenticity and aura: A Benjaminian approach to tourism. *Annals of Tourism Research*, 39 (1), 269–289.

Rorty, R., 1991. *Objectivity, relativism, and truth*. Cambridge: Cambridge University.

Rosaldo, R., 1989. Imperialist nostalgia. *Representations*, 26, 107–122.

Russell, B., 1912 [1971]. *Problems of philosophy*. Oxford: Oxford University.

Said, E., 1989. *Orientalism*. London: Pantheon Books.

Sakwit, K., 2021. *Globalization, tourism and simulacra: A baudrillardian study of tourist space in Thailand*. London: Routledge.

Sands China Ltd., 2020. *Annual Report 2019*. Available from: https://investor.sandschina.com/system/files-encrypted/nasdaq_kms/assets/2020/04/29/7-10-23/1a_2019%20Annual%20Report_ENG.pdf.

Schütz, A., 1967. *The phenomenology of the social world*. Evanston, IL: Northwestern University.

Shi, T. (Tiana), Jin, W. and Li, M., 2020. The relationship between tourists' perceptions of customized authenticity and loyalty to guesthouses in heritage destinations: An empirical study of the world heritage of Lijiang Old Town, China. *Asia Pacific Journal of Tourism Research*, 25 (11), 1137–1152.

Shijiezhichuang, 2023. Available from: www.szwwco.com/en/

Sontag, S., 1979. *On photography*. Harmondsworth: Penguin.

Sorkin, M., 1992. See you in Disneyland. *In*: M. Sorkin, ed., *Variation on a theme park*, New York: Hill and Wang.

Spiegel Reise, June 2012. China presents the replica McBucky' [China weiht nachgebautes Alpendorf ein]. *Spiegel.de*. Available from: www.spiegel.de/reise/aktuell/hallstatt-kopie-china-eroeffnet-nachbau-eines-oesterreichischen-dorfs-a-836618.html.

Splendid China, n.d., Information disclosure [Xinxi gongkai]. *szjxzh.com.cn*. Available from: www.szjxzh.com.cn/list_21.html.

Staples, M., 1995. Heritage tourism and local communities. *Rural Society*, 5 (1), 35–40.

Statista, 2023a. Travel and tourism industry's share of GDP in China from 2014 to 2021, by direct and total contribution. Available from: www.statista.com/statistics/249794/contribution-of-chinas-travel-and-tourism-industry-to-gdp/

Statista, 2023b. Number of outbound visitor departures from China 2010–2021. Available from: www.statista.com/statistics/1068495/china-number-of-outbound-tourist-number/

Street, F., 2020. How the village that inspired 'Frozen' is dealing with overtourism. *CNN*, Jan 10.

Su, J., 2021. The concept of authenticity in cultural heritage Tourism: From separation to interaction [Wenhua yichan lvyou Zhong de zhenshixing gainian: Cong fenli dao hudong]. *Journal of Southwest Minzu University (Humanities and Social Sciences Edition)*, 11, 44–51.

Su, X., 2022. Research on digitalized protection and tourism development of traditional villages [Chuantong cunluo shuzihua baohu yu lvyou kaifa tanjiu]. *Beauty Times*, 6, 76–78.

Sun, P., 2020. *A study on the relationship between the authenticity perception of cultural production, place attachment and behavioral intention: Taking Shenzhen Gankeng Hakka town as an example' [Wenhua shengchan yuanzhenxing ganzhi, defang yilian yu xingwei yixiang de guanxi yanjiu – yi Shenzhen Gankeng kejia xiaozhen weili]*. Thesis (Master's). Jinan University.

Taylor, J.P., 2001. Authenticity and Sincerity in Tourism. *Annals of Tourism Research*, 28 (1), 7–26.

Taylor, P. and Harris, J.L., 2008. *Critical theories of the mass media*. London: McGraw Hill.

The State Council, September 2018. Strategic planning for rural revitalization (2018–2022) [Xiangcun zhenxing zhanlue guihua (2018–2022)]. *www.gov.cn*. Available from: www.gov.cn/gongbao/content/2018/content_5331958.htm.

Tian, M., 2005. Tourists' perspectives on the authenticity of ethnic performance: A case study of Dai minority in Xishuangbanna [Youke dui gewu lvyou chanpin zhenshixing pingpan yanjiu – Yi Xishuangbanna daizu gewu weili]. *Journal of Guilin Institute of Tourism*, 16 (1), 12–19.

Trilling, L., 1972. *Sincerity and Authenticity*. Cambridge, MA: Harvard University Press.

TripZilla, April 2015. China has an exact Replica of the Austrian town of Hallstatt. *trpzilla.com*. Available from: www.tripzilla.com/china-has-an-exact-replica-of-the-austrian-town-of-hallstatt/19481.

UNESCO, 2003. Text of the convention for the safeguarding of the intangible cultural heritage. Available from: https://ich.unesco.org/en/convention

Urry, J., 1990a. The consumption of "tourism". *Sociology*, 24, 23–35.

Urry, J., 1990b. *The tourist gaze: Leisure and travel in contemporary societies*. London: Sage.

Urry, J. and Larson, J., 2011. *The tourist gaze 3.0*. London: Sage.

van den Berghe, P.L., 1980. Tourism as ethnic relations: A case study of Cuzco, Peru. *Ethnic and Racial Studies*, 3 (4), 375–392.

Walby, K. and Piché, J., 2015. Staged authenticity in penal history sites across Canada. *Tourist Studies*, 15 (3), 231–247.

Walton, J., 1978. *The Blackpool Landlady*. Manchester: Manchester University Press.

Wang, J. and Wu, C., 2013. A process-focused model of perceived authenticity in cultural heritage tourism. *Journal of China Tourism Research*, 9 (4), 452–466.

Wang, N., 1999. Rethinking authenticity in tourism experience. *Annals of Tourism Research*, 26 (2), 349–370.

Wang, N., 2001. The mapping of Chinese postmodernity. *In*: A. Dirlik and X. Zhang, eds., *Postmodernism and China*. Durham: Duke University.

Wang, Y., 2007. Customized authenticity begins at home. *Annals of Tourism Research*, 34 (3), 789–804.

Wang, Y. and Chen, Y., 2020. Construction of soundscape in authentic tourism experience – A case study of Dong village in Zhaoxing [Benzhenxing lvyou tiyanzhong shengyin jingguan de goujian – Yi Guizhou Zhaoxing dongzhai weili]. *Huaqiao University Journal (Philosophy and Social Sciences)*, 5, 41–52.

Wang, Y. and Chen, Y., 2022. Research on tourism culture communication strategy of replicative ethnic village – A case study of Yunnan ethnic village [Fuzhixing minzu cunzhai de lvyou wenhua chuanbo celue yanjiu – Yi Yunnan minzucun weili]. *Art Research*, 5, 138–140.

Wang, X., 2021. Study on the relationship between tourist motivation, perception of authenticity and Satisfaction in intimated old city: A case study of Shuihu Haohan Town [Fang gucheng youke lvyou dongji, zhenshixing ganzhi he manyidu guanxi yanjiu – Yi Shuihuhaohancheng weili]. *Tourism Overview*, 5, 131–133.

Wang, Z., 2022. On the expulsion of traditional culture authenticity in the process of tourism development [Qiantan lvyou kaifa guocheng Zhong chuantong wenhua zhenshixing quzhu xianxiang]. *National Circulation Economy*, 3, 126–128.

Waterman, A.S., 2007. On the importance of distinguishing hedonia and eudaimonia when contemplating the hedonic treadmill. *American Psychologist*, 62 (6), 612–613.

Wu, V., June 2012. Made in China: An Austrian village. *Reuters.com*. Available from: www.reuters.com/article/uk-china-austria-idUSLNE85301M20120604.

Xiao, Y. and Li, W., 2022. Research on the renewal strategy of traditional village under the concept of co-governance and sharing: A case of Huitong ancient village in Zhuhai' [Gongzhi gongxiang linian xia chuantong cunluo gengxin celue yanjiu – Yi Zhuhai shi Huitong gucun weili]. *City Architecture*, 10, 18–21.

Xie, P.F., 2003. The bamboo-beating dance in Hainan, China: Authenticity and commodification. *Journal of Sustainable Tourism*, 11 (1), 5–16.

Xie, P.F. and Wall, G., 2002. Visitors' perceptions of authenticity at cultural attractions in Hainan, China. *International Journal of Tourism Research*, 4 (5), 353-366.

Xinfeng County Bureau of Culture, Radio, Film, Tourism and Sports, May 2021a. Notice on printing and distributing the "14th Five-Year Plan" (2021–2025) for Xinfeng County's Culture, Radio, Television, Sports, Culture and Tourism

Industry and Health Industry [Guanyu yinfa <Xinfeng xian wenhua guangdian tiyu shiye, wenlv chanye ji kangyang chanye "shisiwu" guihua (2021–2025 nian)> de tongzhi]. Available from: www.xinfeng.gov.cn/sgxfwgj/attachment/0/125/125652/2042158.pdf.

Xinfeng County Bureau of Culture, Radio, Film, Tourism and Sports, April 2021b. Yunji mountain old town [Yunjishan guzhen]. *sg.gov.cn*. Available from: www.sg.gov.cn/sgly/yzsg/shyj/content/post_1989275.html

Xinhua, June 2012. Controversy caused by Guangdong Huizhou's replication of Austrian town into tourist site' [Guangdong Huizhou fuzhi aodili xiaozhen cheng lvyou jingdian. Yinfa Zhengyi]. *huanqiu.com*. Available from: https://go.huanqiu.com/article/9CaKrnJwzG8).

Yan, C., 2020. The authentic locality: Discussion on the heritage tourism in modern cities [Zhenshi de defang: Dui xiandai chengshi yichan lvyou de tantao]. *Ningxia Social Sciences*, 6, 209–216.

Yan, L., Gao, B.W. and Zhang, M., 2017. A mathematical model for tourism potential assessment. *Tourism Management*, 63, 355–365.

Yan, L. and McKercher, B., 2013. Travel culture in Eastern Jin China (317–420AD): The emergence of a travel culture of landscape appreciation. *Annals of Tourism Research*, 43, 20–36.

Yang, L. and Wall, G.G., 2009. Authenticity in ethnic tourism: Domestic tourists' perspectives. *Current Issues in Tourism*, 12 (3), 235–254.

Yoshimoto, M., 1994. Images of empire: Tokyo Disneyland and Japanese cultural imperialism. *In*: E. Smoodin, ed. *Disney discourse: Producing the magic kingdom*. New York: Routledge.

Zhang, W., 2022. Research on digitalized protection and tourism communication of huizhou folk dance [Huizhou minus wudao shuzihua baohu ji lvyou chuanbo yanjiu]. *Chizhou Collect Journal*, 36 (2), 98–100.

Zhang, Y. and Lee, T.J., 2020. Alienation and authenticity in intangible cultural heritage tourism production. *International Journal of Tourism Research*, 24 (2), 1–15.

Zhong, L., Jinyang, D. and Baohui, X., 2009. Overseas Chinese town: A case study of the interactive development of real estate and tourism. *In*: C. Ryan and G. Huimin, eds., *Tourism in China: Destination, cultures and communities*. London: Routledge, 88–98.

Zhou, N. and Yu, K., 2004. The urbanization of national park and its countermeasures. *Urban Planning Forum*, 1, 57–61.

Zhou, Y., Wu, M., Zhou, Y. and Zhu, Y., 2007. Theory of "authenticity" and its comparison in tourism study [Lvyou yanjiu Zhong de "zhenshixing" lilun jiqi bijiao]. *Tourism Tribune*, 22 (6), 42–46.

Zhu, T. and Lu, L., 2005. Progress of research on cultural tourism in the past decade – A research review of "tourism management", "annals of tourism research" and "tourism tribune"' [Jin 10 nian wenhua lvyou yanjiu jinzhan – "tourism management," "annals of tourism research," and "tourism tribune"]. *Tourism Tribune*, 6 (20), 82–88.

Zhu, Y., 2012. Performing heritage: Rethinking authenticity in tourism. *Annals of Tourism Research*, 39 (3), 1495–1513.

Zhu, Y., 2015. Cultural effects of authenticity: Contested heritage practices in China. *International Journal of Heritage Studies*, 21 (6), 594–608.

Zhuhai National Hi-techIndustrial Development Zone, July 2020. Huitong community will blossom brilliantly. Rural revitalization arena showcases "The most beautiful countryside in Zhuhai"' [Huitong shequ jiang jingcai zanfang Xiangcun zhenxing daleitai jinqing zhanshi "Zhuhai zuimei xiangcun]. *Zhuhai-hitech.gov.cn*. Available from: www.zhuhai-hitech.gov.cn/gxxw/mtkt/content/post_2616099.html

Zou, B., 2021. Factors influencing tourists' travel intention: An analysis based on the theory of planned behavior' [Youke lvyou yixiang yingxiang yinsu – Jiyu jihuaxing-wei lilun de fenxi]. *Social Scientist*, 7, 40–45.

Index